I Am What I Am

I Am What I Am

THE AUTOBIOGRAPHY OF
FRANK 'FOO FOO' LAMMAR
WITH IAN PENNEY AND PETE SMITH

Published by John Blake Publishing Ltd, 3 Bramber Court,
2 Bramber Road, London W14 9PB, England

First published in hardback in 2002

ISBN 1 904034 09 8

British Library Cataloguing-in-Publication Data: A catalogue record
for this book is available from the British Library.

Design by ENVY

Printed and bound in Great Britain by CPD (Wales)

1 3 5 7 9 10 8 6 4 2

Papers used by John Blake Publishing Ltd are natural, recyclable products
made from wood grown in sustainable forests. The manufacturing processes conform
to the environmental regulations of the country of origin.

This book is dedicated to the memory of my loving mum and best friend Leah and to all my family, friends and fans, who have remained loyal to me throughout the years.

ACKNOWLEDGEMENTS

Without question(and with my memory being what it is these days!)this book would never have been started – never mind finished – without the help of the following people: Ian Penney and Pete Smith, for not only coming up with the idea in the first place, but also for the countless hours spent researching and trying to make some kind of sense of my recollections; and to my long-standing and trusted friends Rusty King, Susie Mathis, Colin Rigby and Michael Ryan, for filling in the gaps and for always being there when I needed them.

Contents

MANCHESTER UNITED

The Manchester United Football Club plc, Trafford Training Centre, Birch Road
off Isherwood Road, Carrington, Manchester M31 4BH

I was delighted to be asked to write the foreword for Frank's book.

I have known Frank since I came to Manchester almost 15 years ago. He is one of Manchester United's most staunch supporters and loyal friends and throughout the years he has forged strong relationships with many of the club's players. You can always count on Frank to lend a hand when it comes to charity fundraising.

The charity closest to his heart is the Wallness Children's Charity, for which he has been patron for 18 years. The Royal Manchester Children's Hospital has also benefitted greatly from the fundraising activities of Frank and his many celebrity friends. In fact, there is probably not a charity in Manchester that hasn't been touched by Frank's generosity over the last 30 years.

Frank is a larger-than-life character with a heart of gold, and I can't wait to read about his life. Most of what there is to know about Frank is in these pages, but even that is not enough to describe him: there are parts of this amazing man that only his close friends will be able to tell you about. Frank is a flamboyant performer on stage, but behind the performer, there is no more modest man in the city of Manchester.

It has been my privilege to be the beneficiary of his kindness and goodwill but it has also been a pleasure to get to know him as a true and loyal friend. Loyalty is something of the bedrock of Frank's life and people and friends will testify to this. I have experienced that fierce loyalty, as many others have too and we would all bend over backwards to repay that loyalty, such is the force of Frank Lammar.

It is a privilege to pen these words for what I know will be a remarkable book about a remarkable man, but it is an even bigger privilege to know him.

Alex Ferguson

Sir Alex Ferguson C.B.E

Telephone: 0161 868 8700. Facsimile: 0161 868 8855
A subsidiary of Manchester United PLC. Registered office as above. Registered in England No 95489, VAT No. GB 561 0952 51
WWW.MANUTD.COM

The Angel Finds His Voice

$\mathscr{A}$T LAST, I HAVE to reveal my true age; I can keep it a secret no longer. I – Francis Joseph Pearson – was born on Monday, 22 March, 1937 in Crumpsall Hospital, Manchester, under the sign of Aries and just 24 hours after spring had officially sprung. There, the truth is finally out. That should at least give some journalists something to think about for their future columns.

At the time, my family lived in the Ancoats district of the city, a working-class, back-to-back, *Coronation Street*-type of area close to the city centre. Ancoats itself possessed a large and well-respected hospital, one that dealt primarily with accidents (I most definitely wasn't one of those!) and was certainly the place people went to get stitched up after they'd been fighting in the streets on Friday and Saturday nights. Nearby Crumpsall had a maternity unit, hence the short trip for my mum Leah, on the bus, to east Manchester.

Some may find it astonishing that the *Manchester Evening News* (costing one old penny and printed in their offices on Cross Street) failed to mention me in the births column for the whole week that followed my arrival on that snow-covered Monday morning. The nearest I got was an unfortunate Hulme gentleman named James Henry Pearson (no relation) who sadly died aged 46 on the same day I was born. Mind you, with each line in the classifieds costing a shilling, I'm sure my parents felt their hard-earned money would be better spent elsewhere.

In those days £47 would buy you a 1934 Ford 8 in good condition, whilst various pub jobs were on offer for no more than £1 per week. Should Mum and Dad ever be able to afford it, a new three-bed, semi-detached house on Bury Road in Radcliffe would have set them back no more than £495. If only! On the fashion scene, C&A Modes on Oldham Street were offering a flared and fitted coat for 49s 11d, whilst the nearby department store, Lewis's, would gladly relieve you of 3s in exchange for a pair of silk stockings. My mum waited years to get a pair of silk stockings, only to have them pinched by me for the act. I've got great legs and those stockings were the icing on the cake!

And finally, in establishing the Manchester of six months prior to the outbreak of World War II, I come to showbiz. Television was, of course, still a long way off, so millions of people were kept regularly entertained by the pictures and the wireless. Just opened at The Paramount Theatre on Oxford

Street was *Manhattan Madness* starring Jean Arthur and Joel McCrea; those preferring to stay in tuned to Liverpool comedian Robb Wilton and his marvellous bumbling JP character Mr Muddlecombe.

I was the first-born of a family that would eventually comprise four brothers – Tommy (15 April 1939), Jimmy (29 October 1942) and Brian (28 May 1947) are the others – over a ten-year period. To be perfectly honest, I can't remember a great deal about my very early life in Cookson Street, off Butler Street, one of the main streets in Ancoats. I do, however, have very clear memories of my father Charlie who was a rag and bone man. I can remember, even in the very early days, my mother Leah waiting for him to come home pulling his handcart after a hard day's work. If there was ever anything on that handcart that could be worn by any of the boys, Mum would claim it and take it off to the nearby wash-house at New Islington baths. Anything at all that could be used – little shirts, trousers, socks, even shoes, Mum would rescue for us. Although we didn't know it at the time, we were pioneers in recycling. You had to be in those days. Later on, Dad became an 'entrepreneur'; this meant that he progressed from pulling the handcart himself to letting a horse do it for him!

One of the biggest thrills for us back then was seeing a man coming along our street pulling a barrow and selling tea-cakes, barm cakes and crumpets. It was always early on a Sunday morning and I can still remember him advertising his wares at the top of his voice, a bit like the ice-cream man did. Mum would always go out and buy something from him and it really was a treat we all looked forward to. Nowadays, we have butter on crumpets and tea-cakes; back then it was dripping. Every time Mum cooked meat, she would save the juices in a jam jar ready for when the crumpet-man arrived. Anything this man sold we would toast and cover in dripping.

Although Dad undoubtedly loved Mum and the boys – in fact, all the family – he was known as a bit of a character. On more than one occasion he got 'in with the wrong people', especially after a good weighing day, and would go out and get well and truly drunk. Then there'd be murder! When Dad got the horse, he had the opportunity to go further than the neighbouring streets of Ancoats. He'd go regularly to places like Wythenshawe and Sale, progressing also now to the odd bit of scrap iron to go alongside the rags. Many's the time I would go along with him for the ride and I can still see him giving out the brown-and-white stones that women used for keeping their doorsteps spick and span. This was known as 'donkey stoning'. He'd also blow a bugle (which he probably picked up on his rounds) to announce his arrival in the street, and kept little goldfish – like the kind you can get from the fairgrounds today – in a huge glass bowl alongside him.

My job, when the local kids came out with their unwanted rags (which in most cases were only slightly shabbier than the clothes they were actually wearing), was to put my hand inside this bowl and swirl the water around for all I was worth. Then I'd get a small cup and, with great ceremony, lift one of the goldfish out and pour it into a little plastic bag and give it to the kid, sometimes along with a balloon. It took me a while to realise that all these fish were actually dead and my swirling was all a show. To be honest, some of the old clothes we collected had more life in them than those fish! Looking back at those days, I suppose it was the beginnings of my showbiz career.

My dad was described as a 'loveable rogue'. He was a big man – huge, in fact – and had a full crop of thick wavy hair. I took after him in that department. A good friend of the family – Marjorie McManus – once told me a story about Dad coming home from the pub late at night when, not for the first time, he'd had a 'bad pint' and was feeling very unsteady on his legs. Before getting himself into bed, Dad got the kitchen scissors and hacked off huge chunks of his hair. When he came to the next morning, he was absolutely livid and cries of 'Who the bloody hell's done this?' could be heard many houses away. Despite Mum telling him exactly what had happened, Dad had been so drunk he simply couldn't remember any of it.

Dad was also well known for being quite a good singer, one who thought nothing of joining in with the pianist whenever there was one on in the pub. His six brothers were all of a similar character make-up, so I suppose it's a fair assumption to say that the showbiz part of me came out of that side of the family. When they all got drunk together, one of their favourite party pieces at closing time was to roll up their trouser legs, pick up a wooden chair and off they'd go along the street pretending to be a Scottish pipe band. The regulars waved off the band and the landlord waved off his chairs, although at the time he didn't seem to realise this! The local kids loved it and would follow them for ages along the cobbled streets.

As well as his six brothers, Dad also had five sisters, so when he said he came from a big family, he really meant it. No need to ask what the most popular pastime was in that household!

When Mum and Dad were together, there was no questioning the fact that Dad was the boss and what he said had to be done. Some neighbours and friends at the time said they were sure Mum was scared of him. If that was the case, then I honestly can't remember noticing any fear in Mum. Certainly, like most married couples, they had their rows and disagreements, but I don't think there was anything too serious.

Dad used to have a saying, one that I have held true to all my life. He used to say, 'Don't stoop so low to pick so little up.' In other words, if you can't do someone a good turn, don't do them a bad one – just go. For all Dad's bad points, there were also a lot of good ones. I know I haven't been an angel all my life, but I certainly haven't been a devil either. I've always treated people with respect – even when I was really rough and ready – and I expect respect in return. Who knows, if my upbringing had been different – more privileged, if you like – then maybe I would have a different outlook. Nowadays, I treat everybody – whether they be the roughest or the smoothest – in exactly the same way. I'm not bothered whether they've got a million pounds or fifty pence to their name; as long as they don't wish to harm me, I've certainly no wish to harm them. Everybody, regardless of their status, is welcome in my company. The way I am with people has undoubtedly come from my humble beginnings.

If Dad had a saying I've kept throughout my life, then Mum also gave me a piece of advice that I've tried to keep to. She used to say, 'Always put on clean underwear in case you get knocked down in the street.' Fortunately, to this day I've never had to prove this, but I still do it anyway.

During my very early years, Mum was claiming, or at least receiving, some kind of benefit. My parents would often have a row and then Dad would leave the house and we wouldn't see him for weeks. I found out later that he'd spent some time in prison for not paying maintenance. Being the eldest brother, I once went to visit him in Manchester's Strangeways Prison when he was serving three months for non-payment. Another time, I remember he was locked up in the same hotel for fencing stolen property that had been allegedly collected off his round. The kitchen was constantly piled high with all sorts of stuff but, being as naïve as I was back then, I never thought anything of it. Nowadays, of course, I'd know differently.

With money being somewhat scarce, Mum began to do some part-time cleaning for a Jewish lady who ran the shop on the corner of Butterworth Street and Wilson Street, just a short walk from our house. Obviously, this meant leaving the boys to fend for themselves at times and I have vivid memories of one such occasion around Bonfire Night one year when I was ill with German measles. I was lying on the settee when my brother Tommy decided I was the closest thing he'd be getting to Guy Fawkes and promptly set fire to the settee. Tommy got a real battering from Dad for his trouble.

Fortunately, I suffered only very minor burns to the legs but realised I'd been very, very lucky. The house suffered much worse, though, filling quickly with thick, black smoke, bad enough to warrant a visit from both the fire brigade and the police. The street was soon full of neighbours eager to see the free show courtesy of the Pearson family. We didn't have much, anyway, but the settee – even though it was falling apart and its springs were touching the floor – was a complete write-off.

Owing to Mum's thrifty ways (and Gran's ability with a needle) we did own a few splendid peg rugs that were scattered around the house. Gran would sit there on a chair with a stick happily threading together what looked like hundreds of tiny squares of odd material that Mum had cut up from any old clothes and rags that we'd either grown out of or were beyond salvation. In the winter months, these rugs would be thrown over our beds alongside the overcoats. The luxuries of duvets and blankets were not for the Pearsons of Ancoats; or for that matter, many other Ancoats families either. And neither were the luxuries of indoor plumbing – let alone a proper bathroom – known in the little two-up, two-down we lived in. We had a simple bucket upstairs which was the full extent of the toilet facilities during the night, whilst during the day we made use of the outside toilet at the bottom of the yard.

As well as my job swirling fish on the cart for my dad, I was also responsible for cutting up old newspapers and hanging up the sheets on a nail in the toilet. I think the reason I got this job is because I would constantly pore over the newspapers looking for any references to glamour, Hollywood stars and the like. Who knows, maybe even then, at such an early age, I was destined to make a living out of showbusiness. I sometimes think back to the old days and those bits of newspaper in the toilet. When I read some of the rubbish they print nowadays in the tabloid press, I can't help but wonder whether or not we should still use them in the same way!

Those old enough to remember World War II (and its shortages) will no doubt remember ration books. Like millions of other mums, mine had to sort all these out, although when it came to the sweet coupons, she treated these differently. Despite having these coupons, we still couldn't afford the sweets so Mum would sell our coupons to a more affluent neighbour, Mary Hitchin, and then treat us all (there were three boys then) with the proceeds. She used to take us to the first show at the Tower picture house and then afterwards to Marland's Bakers on Butler Street. Marland's was a big, double-fronted shop and sold the most wonderful home-made meat and potato and steak pies, and puddings. This was another treat we all looked forward to and, by going to the pictures as well, it meant Mum also had a bit of a day out.

When we were just a family of two boys, it was always me who helped Mum more than Tommy. I was certainly much more domesticated, whereas Tommy was much rougher. Even though we very rarely had any money to speak of, we invariably had a good table; Mum always made sure we had something to eat. When we did manage to have meat on a Sunday, any leftovers were cut up and on Mondays we'd have what was called 'tater ash', which nowadays goes by the much grander name of potato pie. Whatever it was called, it was basically all the leftovers thrown in a dish with a crust on top. I have to say that although those early days were tough, overall I have very fond memories of them.

I began my education at Corpus Christi school (where I used to scrounge jam from the nuns) on Varley Street in Miles Platting, another working-class district of Manchester not unlike Ancoats, and situated a few minutes' walk up Oldham Road. We didn't do maths – we did sums! I was there from the age of five to eight, and it was during this time that we moved from the house on Cookson Street. I say moved but we were actually evicted; Dad once again fell down with his payments.

We lived for a good while at number 21 Susan Street, just off Rochdale Road in Collyhurst, about a 15-minute walk from the school. I think it was in this house that we had our first family pet, a very affectionate black mongrel dog called Gypsy. Three doors down the street at number 15 lived Marjorie McManus and her family. I played for hours with my brothers and Marjorie's family in their house and, as time went on, both sets of families became very close. Although Marjorie was only ten years older than me, she regularly looked after me, so much so that I eventually christened her my second mum. Marjorie and Mum also got on like the proverbial house on fire. One day they decided to try a henna rinse together, with disastrous results. Although they now both possessed bright orange hair it didn't stop them going out for a drink together that same night. Unfortunately for both of them, Dad happened to call in to the same pub and, not surprisingly, saw them. He was really angry with Mum and ordered (loudly enough for everyone to hear), 'Two glasses of mild for the whores in the corner!' Mum and Marjorie were so upset they ran out of the pub in tears. Maybe some people were right when they said Dad could be very cruel at times.

Right at the top of Susan Street stood Wilcock's, a wood yard and cooper's. The management at Wilcock's were both generous and smart as Bonfire Night came round. Every year, they'd supply the local kids with loads of off-cuts of wood as well as boxes of fireworks, so we could build a bonfire and generally have a good time. They also knew that if they didn't voluntarily give us the wood, the kids were more than capable of breaking into the yard and looting it anyway! This way, both sides were happy and the local constable wasn't called on to perform his duties.

After Collyhurst, Mum then managed to get us a room at the bottom of London Road, out towards Ardwick Green. London Road, of course, is still there but the entrance to the Mancunian Way and its flyover has long since replaced the room we lived in.

On this stretch of London Road, the Co-Op had both a shop and a bakery with four big houses directly opposite their premises. Mum got us a single room in one of the houses owned by an Irish couple – Mr and Mrs O'Brien – and their family who regularly let out rooms in their property. The room we had was right at the top of the house and was accessible only by climbing three flights of stairs; this was after you'd negotiated a flight of steps on the outside as well. In this one solitary room we had a double bed and a little kitchenette. Everybody – there were now four boys – including my mother would sleep in this one room, although things could have been worse had Dad not been a guest of His Majesty again.

Across the road was a narrow, poorly-lit alley that led to the Co-Op bakery and an area where they'd leave their delivery vans parked up overnight against some railings. Many, many times (more often than not on Saturday nights) I would manage to get into these vans and make off with assorted bread and Swiss rolls to take home.

On the same row as the house we lodged in was a paper shop.

By the time I was ten years old, I had a paper round with them. Without fail, I used to get up very early every morning before going to school and deliver the papers. Every day after school I'd go back to the paper shop and start to deliver the evening ones as well.

I can remember delivering papers in the area immediately surrounding the New Royal picture house on Ashton New Road. There was a tiny street at the side of the cinema and in this street lived a dirty, little old woman, known to everyone only as Amy, who, we kids were told, was a witch. I used to deliver to this dark and creepy house, but neither the woman nor the house ever really bothered me. One day I found out she'd died, so naturally I crossed her off my list and carried on delivering to all the other houses.

Weeks later, a solicitor on Ashton New Road sent for me. It turned out that I'd been mentioned in this old woman's will and she'd left me a purse, two brooches and a shawl. To this day, I've still got those two brooches. I don't know if they're worth anything or not, but I thought it was a lovely gesture from a kind old dear who'd never done me any harm. One of these days I'll try and pay the *Antiques Roadshow* a visit and get them valued. I'll certainly liven that show up!

Another of the places I delivered papers to was Grosvenor Street in Ardwick, a street just off London Road. This road back then was full of big, Victorian-style houses, alas, like many others in the area, no longer with us although the street itself still remains. One particularly large house on this road belonged to a man who bred dogs and he would keep anything between 20 and 30 in cages both inside and outside the house at any one time. The dogs would bark ferociously every time I delivered his papers and then, one day, he offered me a job cleaning out the kennels for him. Naturally, I accepted the offer to go alongside my paper round duties as the extra few shillings a week were more than welcome.

I suppose I must have been about 11 at this point, and I always thought the man had some kind of high-ranking military background (everyone called him the Colonel, whether he was one or not), standing as he did always perfectly straight, as well as being the owner of a curly handle-bar moustache.

My father's family used to live in Cottenham Street, just off Upper Brook Street in Brunswick, a real rough-and-tumble area. Most Sundays, we would walk from our one room to see our gran and she had a huge open fire in the front room and always seemed to be struggling trying to replace the oven door that would constantly be falling off its hinges. Gran would regularly get me to run to the nearby local, the Rutland, for a jug full of Chester's bitter and a penny's worth of Irish white snuff for her. Women taking snuff back then was certainly not unusual. Neither, for that matter, was their liking for a drink.

Whilst cooking the Sunday lunch (after she'd mended the oven door again), Gran could easily put away three or four jugs of bitter. After she'd fed everybody, she'd put on her best shawl and scarf and trot off down to the pub where she'd meet up with all her old friends, who, interestingly enough, were all dressed very similarly. Even to this day, I have a very clear picture in my mind of Gran sat outside the pub drinking with all these old ladies.

The only day these old dears weren't at the pub was Monday; that was wash-house day. Like many other grandchildren in the area, I was roped in to offer my help. The kids would follow the grans down to the wash-house and, when the bedding (which was always washed on a Monday) had been neatly folded and parcelled, we'd wheel it down the road in prams to Bowers' Pawn Shop on Ashton New Road. Every week, without fail, the bedding was pawned, only to be reclaimed when the NAB (the National Assistance, later known as Social Security) arrived a few days later. Gran would also take in washing for other folk nearby, those that had part-time jobs or simply just couldn't make it down to the wash-house. My reward for all this pushing through the streets was an occasional jam butty!

I'm sure this can't be true, but I always remember the weather in my younger days being a lot drier and warmer than it is today. It seemed that most people would simply sit outside on their front doorsteps of an evening idly chatting to their next-door neighbours. When the pubs closed, people would regularly walk in groups singing merrily as they staggered home.

The majority of folk were like the Pearson family, although there were some who had money. These we called 'posh'. When I say money, what I actually mean is that, more than likely, their father was holding down a steady job; they didn't receive free clothes from 'the Education' or money from the NAB. Mr and Mrs Wilkinson were one such family, and Mrs Wilkinson would give me some toffee or a bit of chocolate in return for me singing for her. She'd stand me on a little stool and I would give her a couple of choruses of 'The ash grove how graceful,

How graceful 'tis keeping' in a very high soprano, girl's voice. Mrs Wilkinson loved it.

If the Wilkinsons didn't trouble 'the Education' for their clothing, the Pearsons certainly did. In order to supplement whatever Mum could rescue (sorry, recycle) from Dad's handcart, she'd take us down to the Education Committee on Deansgate, a building that later became the Registrar's Office. There she would get us kitted out with corduroy trousers, a corduroy jacket, a couple of shirts and jumpers, socks and, finally, a pair of clogs. I hated these clogs; they were the ones known as 'sparkin' clogs'. I hated the noise they made as you walked down the street in them and I was strong-minded enough not to wear them. I never had a pair for very long before I pulled the irons off them.

When I was 13 and we were still living in Ardwick, my brother Tommy, who at the time would have been 11, was building up a reputation as being a bit of a 'villain'. Nothing too serious – things like stealing washing off clothes lines – and in the end he was sent to a boys' home in Formby near Southport. It broke my mother's heart because, no matter how little money we had, she was determined to keep the family together. Tommy spent quite a few of his early teenage years at various institutional schools until he was 16, when he got a job down the pit.

And yet, if Tommy was certainly the leader, he wasn't necessarily the sole 'villain' of the family. On more than one occasion, I'd follow him and join him in whatever bit of mischief he was up to and, for some unknown reason, it always seemed to be him and never me who was either caught or at least got the blame. Tommy often used to say if he knew how I managed to get away with things, he'd have done it as well.

Whenever we stayed at Gran's, we'd always be out until one or two o'clock in the morning and have to sneak back in through the trapdoor that led down into the coal cellar. We used to try and beg, steal or borrow whatever we could and the fair on nearby Ardwick Green was always a good place for 'rich pickings'.

The pair of us used to steal fruit fairly regularly from the barrows near to Lewis's on Market Street. Once we'd made our getaway, we'd hide ourselves in the hollowed-out statue of Queen Victoria in Piccadilly Gardens where we'd count up and divide our loot. When we fancied a change of scenery from Manchester city centre, we would take the train out to Altrincham to see what was on offer there. More often than not, these illegal trips were taken when we should have been at school. The thought of paying for these trips never once entered either of our heads.

Another 'crime' we committed took place in Mansfield Street school just around the corner from my gran's house on Cottenham Street. Tommy and I broke in one weekend and were making off with some brand-new football kit when I thought I'd have a bit of fun by ringing the playground bell as loudly as I could. Some said I was a bit cocky in those days (as well as stupid) because, whilst I was making all this noise, I never realised someone else might hear it. Of course, obviously they did and within minutes we were surrounded by neighbouring kids and the police. Fortunately for me, I managed to get away but Tommy wasn't as lucky – again. This time he got locked up for a month in a remand home in Cheshire.

With us not knowing when we'd see Dad again on a regular basis (or Tommy for that matter) the onus fell more and more on me to be the head of the family, although that was easier said than done. Looking back at all the things Tommy and I used to get up to, and the fact that Dad was away a lot, I often think how hard it was for Mum and wonder how she managed to cope. No question about it, we were a pair of little buggers!

I'd been christened a Catholic at Corpus Christi, but the enforced move to Ardwick meant it was too far to walk to the Catholic school and so I moved to St Luke's, which was a Protestant school. It was when I was at St Luke's that I, like many thousands of other kids at the time, walked 'with the scholars' during Whit Week. I distinctly remember one particular year walking down Oldham Street in the city centre and seeing my Dad standing in a pub doorway with his arm round a big, fat woman with blonde frizzy hair. It most certainly wasn't Mum! How I managed to complete the walk I'll never know. All I could think about was getting hold of that woman and doing her some damage.

When the walks had finished, I went back to Oldham Street and, still not knowing exactly what I was going to do, went inside the pub where it seemed to me everyone was drunk. Once inside, I found a box of matches on a table, lit one of them and promptly sneaked up behind this woman and set fire to her hair. Because she had so much lacquer on it, her hair frizzed up even more and she turned around quickly and was all set to smack me when Dad jumped in to save the son who'd just tried to torch his floozy. Fortunately, he'd recognised me and, before the woman could lay a hand on me, he'd given her such a slap she fell off her stool and on to the floor. To this day, I sometimes wonder whatever happened to that woman.

Dad was undoubtedly a good-looking man and he knew it and used his looks to charm the ladies, as Mum used to say, 'Boys will be boys … and so will middle-aged men.' I can prove this first-hand from some of the things I see in my club. Even though he was 'one of the boys', he would always come back home to Mum, although these reconciliations never seemed to last very long and he'd be on his way again shortly afterwards. Mum, though, was completely the opposite. She was most certainly a one-man woman and would never even dream of going with anyone apart from Dad. Mum knew she had the kids to look after and she never once let us down.

We finally left the one room on London Road and moved in with my other gran (Mum's mother, Mrs Florence Hayers) in her house on Butterworth Street in Bradford, Manchester. Interestingly enough, at the other end of this street lived Bill Tarmey, a man later to find great fame as *Coronation Street*'s Jack Duckworth.

The new address meant another school for me; this time it was St Brigid's Roman Catholic, and travelling to and fro was no problem – the school was only about 50 yards from Gran's house! The school was unusual because it was divided into two by the road (the boys on one side and the girls on the other), and a married couple – Mr and Mrs Lofthouse – were the respective headteachers.

Somehow, Gran held down a cleaning job at Ancoats

Hospital, a job she wasn't really physically capable of doing, but nevertheless she did it because she knew the money would come in handy for her daughter and the boys.

The move coincided with another one of Dad's absences. When he was missing, he was either in Strangeways or living with one of his many lady friends. There was one particular woman – Rosie Denoy was her name – with whom Dad spent a lot of time, although, to be fair, she would constantly pester Dad, even when he was back living at home with us. Rosie would regularly go looking for Dad in his local and I developed a fierce hatred for her. She had a young son and had the audacity to call him Charles Pearson after my father, although I knew for certain Dad wasn't the father. He couldn't have been; he was locked up in Strangeways at the time. Even if he did write passionate love letters, there was no way he could be responsible for fathering a child!

Dad's absences caused many arguments within the family. I suppose it could be said that I was tied to Mum's apron strings more than my other brothers, but it certainly seemed to affect me a lot more than it did them. I could see and feel the hurt he was inflicting on Mum. For all of Dad's 'indiscretions', he undoubtedly loved us and, when we were with him, he would have given us his last penny. However, when he'd had a few drinks, it made him into a different person. When he was with the lads, he became one of the lads and my maternal gran hated him for it and the way he treated Mum.

Not surprisingly, whilst at school I, too, became a bit of a ruffian, and one of the things I did there was learn how to box. I was fighting one day inside the school with another lad called

Terry McDermott, when the teacher caught us and told us if we wanted to fight we could do so but only with the gloves on. Not long afterwards they'd set up a makeshift ring in the school yard and I went into this contest with my trousers held up by a piece of string, hidden for appearances' sake, under my jumper. Anyway, this string snapped and, before I knew it, my trousers were round my ankles. The other kids fell about laughing and gave me lots of stick for days afterwards.

In 1992, I was asked by the *Manchester Evening News*, 'What was my embarrassing moment?' I said then that it was this incident when my trousers fell down. It still is today.

Something else I did at St Brigid's was to sing more formally than I'd done in the past. One of the teachers – Mr McDonahue, who, I believe, is still alive today, although by now must be well into his nineties – developed my soprano voice. We used to go to Benediction at St Brigid's Church on Mill Street, which was literally right next to the school, and Mr McDonahue would stand me on a little stool and get me to sing in front of everybody. He then carried this on into the school itself, a practice that only gave the other kids more opportunities to take the mickey out of me because of my high-pitched, girlish voice. I got into more than a few fights because of comments from other lads who mistakenly thought that because I sang like a girl I'd be a bit soft. Funnily enough, in those days there was never any mention of gays or homosexuals. I'm sure they must have been around at the time, but we didn't even know what the word meant.

I can remember a girl at school called Edna Buckley who was quite a pretty young thing and she held quite a fascination for me. Not in the usual way for teenage boys, you understand. I remember she was exactly the same size as me and had some lovely frocks! Sorry, Edna, but that's how it was!

When I was 15, I had a school friend called Richard 'Ricky' Skelly who lived near the Salvage pub in Collyhurst, which could still be there to this day. Most Sundays, I'd go to Ricky's house and then at lunchtime we'd go round to the pub where the landlord would let me get up and sing. The regulars would have a whip round for me, and it wasn't unusual for me to come away with either three or four shillings at a time; remember that was quite a bit of money in those days. I loved having a bit of money for myself. It meant that not only could I buy things for me, but I could also help Mum and, in turn, get a little something now and again for my brothers. I liked this feeling so much, I began to go back at night-times as well, although I soon realised that people didn't want singing in the evening and consequently weren't as generous with their donations. Mum never knew I was even trying this. At first, I used to leave the house early and be back well before 9.00pm.

This first taste of singing at night took hold of me and I soon began staying out later than the 9.00pm curfew Mum tried to impose. She didn't like the idea, and when she did find out we had a few disagreements about it, but I liked the extra money coming in – it was my 'collection' – as well as the independence. This situation went on for a good few months, and I would always be up for school the next morning.

A lot of my friends when they left school were very brainy. It was well known that I, on the other hand, whilst never being dumb in any way, shape or form, was just not interested in the academic school work and I suppose the teachers knew this and they didn't appear to bother with my education. I did manage to get on the good side of Mr Lofthouse, the headmaster, and became the boy who'd go round with the school dinner tickets and the milk vouchers. I hardly ever joined in with cricket and football (I was never any good at either, anyway) but no one ever made me. I can remember once at St Luke's we played a game of football against another local school but only had ten men. I'd have been about nine at the time and, because I was no good, I was never normally picked for a kickabout, but this time they were left with no choice and had to draft me in. I scored what I thought was a perfectly good goal and began to celebrate but noticed my team-mates didn't seem as pleased as I was. It was then that the penny dropped – I'd scored in the wrong goal! Needless to say, I was on the receiving end of a good few slaps! Even my brother Tommy leapt on my back and gave me a back-hander for my trouble.

As time went on, I did more and more jobs for the headmaster and, with hindsight, I suppose, I became his 'skivvy'. Even though I was trusted with collecting the kids' dinner money, I have to admit to helping myself to some of it occasionally so I could go and buy sweets. At this time Mum used to have a wireless set with an accumulator (a kind of battery that powered the wireless) attached, and when this ran down there was a shop close by that would recharge it for a few pence. I have to admit also that the school dinner money sometimes paid for this recharging as well. No questions were ever asked about these shortages; to be honest, I'm not sure anyone actually checked the amounts in the first place.

There was one particular teacher, however – a former Manchester United footballer called Lawrence Cassidy, who disliked me at the time, although we got on better in later years – who took it upon himself to make an example of me in front of the whole school. The final straw for him was when he saw me one day wearing my clogs, minus the irons, which I'd removed previously as usual. Once again, I was placed on a stool in front of the whole school, only this time instead of singing, Mr Cassidy proceeded to tell everyone I'd abused the fact that the education system was clothing me and the money was coming out of his and every other hard-working tax-payers' pockets. I was so embarrassed I ran out of the school immediately and back home to Mum.

My sudden return home also coincided with one of Dad's and he was furious with what had happened and was all set to go back to the school and sort Mr Cassidy out. Mum, for her part, was adamant that I was never going back but, in the end, the priest visited the house and things were eventually smoothed over. I suppose what Mr Cassidy had said was right in one respect, but whatever was said, I was determined never to wear irons on my clogs.

Because of my singing voice, other people at the school began to take notice of me, especially at Christmas-time. Midnight mass on Christmas Eve is a big thing in the Catholic Church and I can clearly remember standing there dressed in black and white singing 'Ave Maria' in my very high-pitched voice. Mr McDonahue said to me, 'You've got the voice of an angel, but you can also be a devil.'

Father Fitzgerald was the priest at St Brigid's and, even all those years ago, must have been in his late seventies. Despite his age, he was a man with an amazing memory. He would constantly hang out of his bedroom window over the vestry and shout at kids who he knew (and I don't know how he knew) hadn't been to confession or Benediction. Just for good measure, he'd give you a clip round the earhole when he later saw you face to face. Many's the time I've heard him shout 'Francis Pearson' in his loud, roaring voice. I was frightened to death of Father Fitzgerald, even if he did love my singing.

My Christmases back then were nothing like the ones the kids of today have. When I think of my niece Becky asking for a new pair of trainers recently, the price was something like £60. All we ever got – if we were lucky – was an apple, an orange, a banana and some nuts. Occasionally, we'd get an odd second-hand toy that one of the neighbours would be throwing away. What with being such a large family and the money being tight, we couldn't afford a turkey dinner so Mum, once again, made do. She used to buy two big chickens (as this was cheaper) and then made sure we had all the vegetables so at least we could have a traditional Christmas dinner. The food, coupled with the few crackers she'd bought off the market, made the day's meal different from the others, although financially we were literally a million miles away from the money people spend today. In later life, as I grew older and got involved in showbiz, Christmas for me meant working. It meant making other people happy – works' parties, celebrations and the like. So, in all honesty, I have to say that for various reasons, Christmas is not really one of my favourite times of year, even though I am still a Catholic and have strong beliefs. I prefer New Year if for no other reason than it gives me a little bit of time off, especially the first full week of the New Year when the club scene dies down considerably from the mayhem of the previous month or so. These few days also gave me the opportunity to get the family together and more, often than not, we'll all go out to a restaurant somewhere in Manchester and I'll treat them all to a slap-up meal.

People ask me if I make New Year's resolutions and the simple answer is, 'No, not any more.' I had a spell in the late 1970s and early 1980s when, immediately after the bells had rung at midnight, I'd say, 'Right, this year I'm going to do less. I'm going to cut down on all the charity work, all the clubs, everything.' By 12.15 the bloody phone had rung and someone was saying, 'Frank, any chance you could do such and such a thing for us?', and we'd be off again. So, in the end, I just gave up with the resolutions completely.

As I mentioned earlier, a good friend of mine in my young days (in fact all through my school days) was Ricky Skelly. Ricky had vivid red hair and was a smashing lad who tragically died of a heart-attack whilst still in his forties. Together, we were a real rough pair and Ricky was a brilliant boxer. Even though I never shirked any schoolyard skirmishes – indeed, I could handle myself in most situations – I suppose at times I stood behind Ricky because he was such a good fighter. We were inseparable and used to get up to all kinds of mischief.

One such instance happened in the Jolly Carter pub on Ashton New Road, a regular haunt of my maternal grandmother and just across the road from one of our more regular haunts (albeit it for different reasons), Bowers' Pawn

Shop. Ricky and I would rush into the pub and shout, 'Mrs Hayers, Mrs Hayers,' at the top of our voices and then rush out again and hide behind the nearest corner. Gran would say, 'Who said that?' The reply came back, 'It was two lads and one of them had flaming red hair.' Ricky's colouring had given him away and, of course, everybody knew that wherever he went, I went, and so obviously the other lad was me. Gran used to really batter me when I got back home, thinking all sorts of domestic tragedies had taken place that warranted her leaving the pub and her beer.

A school reunion was held at St Brigid's in August 1987; however, owing to prior commitments, I was unable to attend. It was just one of those unfortunate things, although reading between the lines in one newspaper, it tried to make out that I missed the gathering on purpose. I can assure you nothing was further from the truth. By all accounts, those who did attend had a good time and apparently no one missed me anyway! It also appears that I was mentioned in conversations, though, with my age (again!) and (unfortunate) school nickname of 'Della' being among the topics.

I left school with no formal qualifications aged 15 in 1952, the same year as the young Princess Elizabeth became Queen. Although our lives could not have been more different, our paths would cross many years later to provide me with one of the greatest moments of my life. Back then, amazingly 50 years ago, she knew exactly how her life was planned out. I, on the other hand, had no idea how I was going to earn a living in the big, wide world. Ironically enough, my first job took me back to the very same Co-Op bakery I had stolen from just a few years earlier.

2

Army Camp

I GOT A JOB with the Co-Op as a van boy and would travel around the area with John Heywood, the van driver, helping out with the deliveries. We used to go to leafy, suburban Cheshire, where the big houses of Hale and along Washway Road in Sale seemed to be from a different world to the terraced one I was used to. I would dream regularly about these houses with their fancy cars outside and would say to myself, 'One day, one day, I'm going to have one of those cars and a big house like this.'

John used to say to people that he had the Co-Op's best rep working with him. I had the ability to direct myself towards the customers and talk to them even though I didn't really know I was doing it. The other van boys would just follow the drivers around carrying the baskets of bread saying very little (and only then when spoken to) and certainly never being allowed inside the customers' houses. I, on the other hand, dressed in my brown overall, had this sort of 'camp' style about me and could easily sell the customers more than they intended buying in the first place. Along with the bread deliveries, we also sold cakes in boxes of six and my particular favourites were wimberry tarts. These were little cakes covered in cream and I used to love licking some of the cream off the top of them. Using my finger, I'd then try to cover the gaps with the remaining cream before putting the cakes back in their box. Despite the fact that sometimes my efforts weren't as good as they should have been, my gift of the gab was so good that the customers still bought the cakes anyway.

We did the same round every week, and consequently I got to know some people very well. One round was Monday, Wednesday and Friday, and the other was Tuesday, Thursday and Saturday. The people we delivered to were very nice and kind towards me, some of them even gave me some old clothes their kids had grown out of and even an occasional parcel to take home to my mum.

I was now 16, and after the round I'd walk home each night from the bakery along London Road towards Ashton New Road. There were two pubs on opposite corners to each other on London Road – the Robin Hood and the Bull's Head, a pub which is still standing today and is now directly opposite the new entrance to Piccadilly Railway Station. Most nights as I'd be walking past the Robin Hood, I would hear a piano playing and people singing inside. I loved the singing and I'd stop on the street to listen for a few minutes each time I walked by, desperately wanting to go inside, but I never did.

One particular night as I was standing outside, a man came out of the pub carrying a music bag and said to me, 'I've seen you standing here before many times.'

'I know,' I replied, 'I want to sing.'

He went on to ask me how old I was and where I lived. When I told him I was 16 and lived up Ashton New Road, he said he played on Ashton New Road, in the Prince of Wales pub on the corner of Forge Lane, right next to Johnson's Wire Works. Of course, I knew exactly where this was, living close by in Butterworth Street, and we continued to chat for a few minutes.

Anyway, we parted and I set off for home, thinking that was the end of that, but one Sunday a few weeks later I thought I'd go and try to find this man again and set off for the Prince of Wales. Inside the pub entrance was a lobby area with a small serving hatch, and then off to the side was a room with a piano. There, sat at the piano, was the man I was searching for. Coincidentally his name was Eric Pearson, although, as it turned out, he was no relation. Eric was a bald-headed man who played the piano for a hobby in his spare time; during the day, he was employed by Lewis's as an electrician.

Eric saw me standing in the doorway and immediately called me over to him. Next to the piano was a microphone and Eric said to me, 'What do you want to sing then?' Taken aback by this sudden request, I said I didn't know and Eric then asked me, 'Well, what *can* you sing?' I said I knew, 'On the Street Where You Live' from the musical *My Fair Lady*, and he simply said, 'Right, sing that then.'

Well, I did, and all the old women – dressed in their uniform of shawls and scarves – seemed to like it and so it became the first song I ever sang in public, apart from either at school or in the choir. After I'd finished the song, Eric asked me if I knew both my mum and gran frequented the pub, especially on ladies' darts nights. I said I didn't, although I did know Gran would take Mum out for a drink some nights by way of a little treat for her.

Marion Worley was the landlady of the Prince of Wales and she came over to see me. 'You know you shouldn't be in here, don't you?' she said to me. Because I knew I was under-age, I replied defensively, 'But I haven't had a drink.' She said, 'I know, but still. Anyway, I do like your singing.' At that, I plucked up the courage to ask her if I could come back. She said she'd first check with my mother and, as long as it was OK by her, then the answer was 'Yes'. I assume she did clear it with Mum, because when I went back again two weeks later, no one seemed to bat an eyelid and so began a regular Sunday event for me.

A few weeks later, I received my first 'wage' – and I still class it as a wage – for singing. It was five shillings! When Mrs Worley gave me the money, I thought it was fantastic; I just couldn't get over it. My wages at the bakery at this time were about £6 a week, an amount I'd take home to Mum still in its unopened pay packet. I also gave the five shillings to her to help towards paying the clubmen.

One of these was a man called Brown who had a clothes shop and would call regularly to people's house to collect money which was then set aside for later purchases. Mum always insisted we had new clothes for Whit Week and would scrimp and save towards this goal but, more often than not, found herself short when the time arrived. Mum also found herself involved with 'the loan woman'. This was someone who'd always be prepared to lend a struggling family, say, £20 or £30, but would always want £30 or £40 in return. When these debts were taken alongside the regular trips to Bowers' Pawn Shop (which, as well as the family bedding, now included my best sports coat and trousers every Monday), you can see just how scarce money was for us in the early 1950s and my singing money went some way to helping Mum. Every Friday, it was back to Bowers' for my mum with a few bob in order to get my things out in readiness for singing again at the weekends.

It would have been around the same time as I was at the Prince of Wales that I got my first compèring job, at the Bakers' Union Club in Moss Side, working alongside Eric the organist, who, I believe, passed on a few years ago. I'd already done some spots there previously as a singer, and then one night they asked me if I fancied the compère's job, so, always up for a challenge, I said 'Yes'.

Most of the audience were a lot older than me, but that didn't bother me in the slightest as I was still learning the ropes and was willing to have a go at most things as long as there was an audience around. I mean that in the true showbiz sense only! With hindsight, I suppose it was a good training ground for what was to come.

When I reached my seventeenth birthday, Marion and her

husband, landlord Dick, told me they were going to lay on a party for me at the pub and I distinctly remember it being on a Sunday. They made some sandwiches and the like and I was the star of the show. Everyone who came that evening had come to hear me sing.

That was probably the first 'proper' birthday I can remember. Up to that point (similar to Christmases, really) we used to make do with what we could get for birthday treats. I can't honestly remember getting any presents as such, certainly not as children nowadays expect. I'd never really looked forward to my birthdays, so I treated them as just another day. It was from this day, and certainly later when I became a better known figure in showbusiness, that I genuinely looked forward to my birthdays, knowing that something different was going to happen.

A regular local event around the time of my seventeenth birthday was the landladies' night out. This was when three or four landladies from nearby pubs all got together and would spend a social evening in one of their premises. The following week it would be someone else's turn, and so on. My singing was proving so popular in the Prince of Wales that Marion asked me to do a regular Wednesday spot as well as the Sundays. It was on Wednesdays that the landladies had their get-togethers and, when they saw me, they began to ask me to sing for them in their pubs when I wasn't on at the Prince of Wales. Mind you, I suppose you could say I became almost part of the furniture at the Prince of Wales in the end. I must have been there for something like four years and was such a success that Dick and Marion even had some special toffees made which customers could buy as souvenirs. These were a kind of caramel and were sold in boxes – with my name on, no less – behind the bar.

Whether it was a Tuesday, Thursday or whenever they had their pianist on, I would go and sing at other pubs – the Forge and the Commercial spring to mind immediately as two pubs I performed in regularly. As time went on, I developed a kind of circuit, if you like, and really looked forward to my evening's work.

While all this was going on, I was still working at the bakery in the daytime but the long walk to and from home in Ardwick was by now getting to me. Although I still liked the work itself, I decided it was time for a change and got a job in Lawson's cotton mill on Butler Street, close to Oldham Road, in Ancoats. My first job at Lawson's was bagging the waste and, not long after I started, I began to tell the girls tales of my 'glamorous life in the world of showbiz'. For them, it made a pleasant change from the everyday drudgery of millwork and they all seemed to enjoy me telling the stories. It was my first experience of being in contact with a room full of women for any length of time. It was an experience that would stand me in good stead in the coming years.

All I was interested in outside of work was dressing up and being somebody, although I never knew then what it would all lead to. Some people might say that I would eventually make a living out of my hobby! I would go regularly to school dances in my teens and will never forget one trip I made with my mum to the market on Grey Mare Lane in Beswick searching for some new shoes to go out in. I'd been to the market previously and had seen this beautiful pair of brown bedroom slippers on a second-hand stall. They were such a lovely pair of shoes that I'd convinced myself that even though they were bedroom slippers they looked as good as a pair of slip-on shoes and, as such, could be worn very smartly and confidently outside. Mum bought these for me for 1s 6d and, as time went on and the brown began to discolour and fade, I died them black with boot polish and continued to wear them. They, along with a brand-new pair of jeans, became my pride and joy.

I'd been at the cotton mill for about 12 months as Christmas approached when it was decided that a lunchtime party was to be put on for the workers in the canteen. It was nothing fancy, just all the girls having the opportunity to let their hair down and have a few drinks and, as they knew I did some singing in the evenings, I was asked if I'd get up and sing for them. This was another first for me; it was the first time I'd ever been up on a big stage.

I feel sure that around this time, what with the singing in the pubs and the close working with the girls in the mill, that the early seeds of 'Foo Foo' were sown. Even though I was still only 17 and therefore still just under the legal age limit as far as the pubs were concerned, I was gaining confidence all the time and I began to feel as though what I was doing and, indeed, where I was doing it, was 'legal'. I could quite easily pass for 18 and when I was doing a number on stage it was not unknown for me to wander into the audience, take a scarf off a woman's head and start to camp it up. I found that the more I did that sort of thing, the more I chatted to the audience and got them involved, the more they liked it. I'd say things to the audience (never knowing sometimes where they'd come from) like, 'She's only wearing that scarf because she's got nits.' I used to judge people on what I saw and told them accordingly and this camp style just took me over. Along with the scarf, I'd often pick up one of their handbags (in those days, it always seemed to be a huge, brown thing with two handles and no doubt full of pawn tickets) and would go off poncing around the room with it. I really enjoyed doing it as much as the women seemed to like me doing it.

Dick Worley, the landlord of the Prince of Wales could see how much I loved to sing and one day suggested to me there might be a way to spread my wings a bit further. Not too far from the market on Grey Mare Lane was the Bradford Labour Club, the regular Sunday meeting place of all the club concert secretaries (the guys who book the acts) in the area. Dick suggested I should go along with him one particular Sunday lunchtime as he'd arranged to put my name down for a talent contest where I could get up and give them a song. I remember going into this big room and seeing some familiar faces in the audience who, in turn, recognised me, and I sang in front of an organist and a drummer, the first time I'd been accompanied by more than one man and a piano. Although it was still just two men, to me it was like having the Royal Philharmonic Orchestra behind me. I was allowed to perform two songs and the reception I received after the first carried me away so much – unwittingly or unknowingly, or maybe even both – I went into my routine of being camp and working the audience like I'd do regularly with the women in the pubs. The place just went up. When I'd finished the second song, the compère came over and said to me, 'You've done four minutes over time there. Nobody ever gets that.' Sheepishly I replied, 'Oh, I'm sorry, I didn't realise.' Even if the compère was less than pleased, the judges weren't bothered; I won the contest outright. For weeks afterwards, I had people (all concert secretaries or their assistants) knocking on our front door on Butterworth Street asking if I could do this club or that club. Mum wondered what the hell was going on at first with all these strangers turning up at different times of the day and night!

I didn't know what had hit me. Much as I was delighted with all these offers my main concern was, 'What am I going to wear?' I certainly had nowhere near enough clothes for all these extra shows. All I had was my sports coat and trousers and these were only available at weekends; remember, the rest of the week they were in the pawn shop. I was determined not to let this get the better of me and even though Mum continued to pawn my 'weekend gear', I began to save really hard, eventually being able to afford to buy a new suit, one that I was certainly never going to allow near the pawn shop. This became my 'stage gear', the first of many such outfits as the years progressed. I bought this suit with a £5 deposit and the rest paid weekly from Sid Vernon, a Czech tailor on Ashton New Road, someone who fortunately knew me and trusted me for the rest of the money. The suit was actually made up of a beige jacket, dark brown trousers and a brown-and-beige shirt with my faithful old slippers completing the ensemble. On top of all this finery, I had a Tony Curtis hairstyle complete with a 'DA'. Looking back, I must have looked like a chocolate blancmange!

When I turned 18 in 1955, like many other young boys then, I left home at the request of the Government and joined the Army to do my National Service. Even though many of you might find this hard to believe, it's true. Remember, back then it was compulsory, you couldn't refuse, and all the neighbours arranged a little party for me in the pub (where Mum had a little cry) just before I left for Oswestry. I was joining the Royal Artillery; I was going to be a gunner. Not a rear gunner ... just a gunner!

I got off the train in Oswestry and was met by a big army sergeant with an even bigger truck and taken off to camp, so to speak. We assembled on parade and were met by a lovely man with a voice like Pavarotti when he was pissed. He yelled at me, 'I see by your hair you think this is for fairies.'

I asked politely, 'What is for fairies?'

He yelled again, 'Call me Sergeant,' continuing, 'that hair has to come off.'

I said, 'Well, if it's coming off, then I'm going home. I'm not having my hair cut.' I still thought I was back home where I always got my own way. Things were not the same now, though, so I got my hair cut. I say cut but it was still long enough for me to do at least a little something with it. I can remember stealing some pipe cleaners from the officers' mess and using them as makeshift hair curlers. I put them in one night just before bedtime but unfortunately for me I failed to wake up and take the things out before the sergeant did his rounds in the morning. To say he wasn't pleased with me was an understatement. Perhaps that was the moment when both the Army and me knew we weren't truly compatible.

I then had problems with the uniform. They gave me a huge pair of boots to wear which felt very strange because I'd never worn boots before. The other thing about them was that they were brown and I was immediately told to polish them black. The uniform itself was very hairy, especially the underpants, and I just couldn't wear them and refused to do so. Although I wasn't used to silk or anything like that, the whole uniform used to make my skin itch. Even though I was frightened to death of the authorities, I stood my ground on this and was determined not to wear them. The sergeant then took me to see the commander of the whole camp, Colonel-in-Chief or whatever he was, who stood proudly in front of me with a chest full of medals. When meeting the Colonel you had to say your name, rank and serial number. The only thing was, I could never remember my number; I used to have it written down on little pieces of paper and stuffed in my pockets. So I went in and said to him, 'Gunner Pearson. Can you hang on a minute while I get my number out?'

His first question to me was, 'What do you feel, son, about being in the Royal Artillery?'

I replied, 'Well, if there was a war on, I suppose I could fight. I'm not daft. I was brought up a bit rough. But I can't be doing with all these hairy clothes and polishing these brown boots black. I can't see the point of getting up so early and doing all this stuff with the bed.' (Every morning we had a full kit inspection when we had to lay all our gear out on the bed. Well, I was used to sleeping four to a bed and I never even *made* the bed, let alone having to put all my gear out on it.) He then asked me what I did at home. When I told him I sang and camped it up in pubs and clubs it made his mind up for him. Within three months, I'd gone in Grade 1 and came out Grade 91. They shipped me out as quickly as possible. Maybe that told me something or other … I'm not sure.

I didn't know what I was going to tell Mum, so I made up a story on the train back home. I told her I'd been hit in the ear by a rifle butt and suffered a perforated eardrum so they had to discharge me. Hit by a rifle! I never even saw one and I certainly couldn't pick one up; they were too heavy! The only good thing about my time in the Army was the passing out parade. I'm sure they just gave me mine because I was the only one who never went on the square. You wouldn't catch me wearing that horrible uniform and prancing up and down in those big boots. Anyway, for this one particular day, the day of the passing out parade, I wore the uniform. There must have been about 6,000 men on that parade ground and I must have been the only one there wearing someone else's boots. The ones I had bloody crippled me and so I had to borrow another pair. The authorities relented a bit as well, though, because they allowed me to wear my own underpants underneath so the material wouldn't rub. I think I've still got a photo of me in uniform somewhere, taken on that day. I stood on the square with my beret stuck on the side of my head trying my best to look like a cross between a French tart and Marlene Dietrich. If they'd have given out Oscars in the Army, then I'd have definitely won one for my performance on that parade ground. The other lads loved it and treated me almost as their mascot. I was the only one brave enough (or daft enough) to do these bizarre things; none of the others had the balls to try them and so they all loved me and would encourage me to do even more.

After the parade, there was a bit of a do in one of the huts and a band had been laid on. Ever the showman, I got up and gave them a song. I sang 'Once I Had a Secret Love', the Doris Day and, later, Kathy Kirby number. Well, it brought the house down; the soldiers loved it and I got a standing ovation.

I understood the need and importance for the country to have armed forces and the like, but I realised that I just wasn't cut out for it. All this marching up and down and boot polishing wasn't for me. I was just wasting my time in the Army. I'd always worked for a living and wondered a lot about what Mum was doing at home without my wages coming in. When I left, I received a pay packet from the Army for the three months. God knows why; I'd certainly not earned anything. I didn't offer it back, though, and the extra few quid would come in handy for when I got home.

I didn't tell Mum the exact day I was returning home. I arrived at Piccadilly Station in the same little suit and scarf I'd left in, and bought some cotton wool on the station. I pushed a ball of it into my ear, just to confirm my 'injury', before setting off for home. That first night back home, we went to the Lord Napier pub on Grey Mare Lane where they were having a darts match and 'tater pie supper. In the end, things changed and the night turned into a 'Welcome Home Frank' night. I didn't crack on about the injury, though; after all, it was just a little white lie. Me in the Army was certainly a most memorable experience. Not necessarily for the right reasons, but nevertheless an experience.

After that party I made a point of staying in the house for the next four or five weeks until my hair grew back. I looked as though I'd been in Strangeways for about six months!

Another memorable thing about my army life was a girl. Yes, a girl! Her name was Alice Smith and she used to write to me regularly whilst I was in Oswestry. I know I wasn't in that long, but she did promise to wait for me. I think some people have waited longer for a bus! I suppose she was hoping I'd come out some high-ranking officer, but in the end I just came out a YTS – or ATS! Anyway, it turned out that the wait wasn't worth it for either of us, and what little 'romance' we had soon petered out. I think she still lives somewhere near Manchester today, and has settled down to a normal family life, so she obviously wasn't too disappointed when things didn't work out between us.

Not long after I left the Army (I don't know who was more glad at my departure, me or the Army), another change of daytime career beckoned. One of the regular ladies in the Prince of Wales, Sylvia Lane, told me there was a job going at the place she worked, Edwin Butterworth's Paper Mill on Pollard Street, still in Ancoats. As well as processing waste paper, Butterworth's also had a good business in recycling old clothes and rags and even had a laundry service for places like workshops and garages.

Sylvia knew I was bagging waste at the cotton mill and also knew, like I did, that it was a bloody awful job. She told me she'd put my name down at her place and, after I'd served my obligatory week's notice at Lawson's, I started at Butterworth's. I'd moved on from bagging waste cotton and was now baling waste paper. There were seven women and me, five days a week, full-time waste paper balers. These women were the like of which you'd never see nowadays. They were big, tattooed women who thought nothing of hurling five or six hundredweight bundles of waste paper and card on to the backs of lorries. I know some women today who struggle to pick up a packet of cornflakes! One woman in particular, I remember, was Vina Hampson. She must have been in her seventies with no thought of retirement, but had arms like a wrestler and could still hurl the paper around as easily as the younger ones. Vina had a daughter, Minnie, who also worked at Butterworth's and a son, Johnnie, who I got to know quite well and even palled out with for a while.

Another older, female baler I remember was Lizzie Anne, and we used to say she was 'posh' because she'd bring her sandwiches to work every day wrapped in a tea towel. Even then she must have been well into her sixties. She was a very stern woman who didn't really know how to take to me at first, but eventually grew to like me and used to say, 'You're very naughty, but very nice.'

One of the best workers we had was known to everyone as Old Mary, a real grafter and one who could rake out six tons of waste paper a lot quicker than most of the other younger girls, but she was terribly dirty. So dirty, in fact, that she had nits and some of the other women refused to work with her. We used to call her 'Greasy Ankles' because her feet were always black. I don't think they ever saw soap and water. What made it even worse was that, because she used to wear second-hand shoes, none of them were ever the right size and consequently these horrible feet were forever on show. She really was a poor soul and owned only the clothes she stood up in. It got so bad that one day I put on a pair of rubber gloves, took her into a bag room and cut all her hair off. I then literally deloused her, rounded up as many decent clothes as I could from the rags we were recycling and then redressed her. I don't think she'd ever looked as good before in her life. Some time later, she trod on a rake and developed a growth on her leg that became infected and eventually killed her. I'm sure if she'd have looked after herself better, this would never have happened.

But it was a different era back then and the women simply had to go out to work because they needed the money. Even though none of us had any money we always tried to have a good social life. I can remember clearly the countless times we'd take empty mineral bottles back to the pub so we could get our 'let in' money. This was usually just enough to let us get our first half of mild or bitter. Once we were in, I'd get up and sing a song and from then on there was always someone who'd buy us a drink. Most lunchtimes we'd run to the pub and have pie and chips and a good old sing-song. It was very rough work but I made the girls laugh a lot and they liked me and the atmosphere was terrific.

On the whole, we had a lot of fun but I well remember a day I was far from laughing. One young lad had gone inside one of the huge presses we had in the factory to do some routine maintenance when somebody outside unknowingly switched it on. The poor lad inside was in a terrible state and I had the misfortune (being one of the few males there) of being chosen to go in and get him out. Fortunately, he somehow survived but it was touch and go for a while.

Edwin Butterworth's was a huge concern and employed somewhere in the region of 400 people, including for a while both my mum and my auntie Mary. I worked with the girls in 'O Department', the waste paper department. Within three years I'd progressed to Foreman, along with 'Irish' Jerry O'Neill – I must have been 22 by then – and took over the whole department including sorting, baling, pressing and the production of the different colours and grades of paper. There must have been something like 90 women working in the department and for a while, apart from Jerry, I was the only lad working with them. I loved every single one of these women and they, in return, loved me. They also taught me everything you could possible want to know about being a woman. I used to love some of their expressions and would incorporate them in later years when Foo Foo came on the scene. They'd say things like 'You tassle tossing tessie' to each other, which, although I'm sure doesn't mean anything, sounds like swearing when you say it quickly. Working with these ladies at Butterworth's was an experience and one I wouldn't have missed for the world.

My immediate manager was Ted McGhee, a very shy and reserved man who, judging from his appearance and personality, you wouldn't have believed worked amongst all these women, tons of waste paper and rags. In spite of first appearances, Ted nevertheless was a lovely man with whom I got on very well.

I was a good worker and got 'well in' with the management at Butterworth's. One of the senior managers, Mr Desmond, used to arrive for work every morning driving a big, swanky car. When I saw this car, it brought back memories of when I was a delivery boy for the Co-Op and I remember saying to Sylvia once, 'I'm going to have a car like that one day.' Admittedly, initially I had to set my sights a little lower, but one day, years later, that recurring dream would come true.

There were two families who ran Butterworth's – the Stansfields and the Tarbucks, both of whom also had sons on the board. Bill Tarbuck (the father) was a very educated and shrewd man who had been brought in from outside the immediate Butterworth family to try and polish the business up. His son Dave was not particularly well liked by the workers, even less than the average director's son is under similar circumstances. I'd come from a completely different background to Bill and he struggled at first really to understand what I was all about, although he did recognise my ability as a good worker and would, as time went on, begin to bounce ideas off me.

He even asked me for my opinion when it was suggested that a time and motion study was to be carried out at the factory. I gave my honest opinion when I told him that it was virtually impossible to do this with such a large workforce of women who were 60 years old and upwards. I don't think I'm being too big-headed when I say I'm sure he valued my opinion. In fact, it could be said that I educated him in the ways of dealing with the kind of people I'm sure he'd never encountered before he came to Butterworth's.

I'd progressed to Foreman when David Stansfield (the other director's son) said to me, 'I'm going to ask my father to promote you. I want you to become Assistant Manager.' Naturally, I was delighted and jumped at the opportunity and the extra money meant I could now buy myself my first vehicle.

One of the companies we dealt with back them was Hadfield's, a Failsworth-based company which regularly delivered waste cardboard boxes to us for recycling. It was from Geoff Hadfield that I bought my first vehicle, an Ellis's meat pie van, still with the gold lettering on the side. Geoff delivered it to me in the yard at Butterworth's and we agreed a price of £30. Again, like my stage suit, because Geoff knew me, he agreed to weekly repayments. Off the record and in return for his generosity, I used to put a bit extra on his load at Butterworth's, but that's another story!

At lunchtimes (and with the help of some of the girls), I painted the van green and would later pass my driving test in that very same vehicle. I was reminded only recently of what actually happened with that van. I was filling it up one night when, instead of putting diesel in, I put in petrol and blew the thing up. Well, I did the best I could; I just left it on the garage forecourt and ran away. I'd had it so long by then it was probably only worth a couple of bob anyway.

One summer, I arranged a day trip for my department, about ten of us in all, to the seaside at Southport and the plan was for all of us to go in my van. We met up at the Auld Lang Syne pub on Pollard Street (not too far from the mill) on the Sunday morning when the landlord agreed to open the doors for us at 10.30am. However tragedy was to strike – I had two flat tyres on the van. Well I could only see one alternative. I went back to the mill, opened the yard gates and brought the waste paper van out. With it being a Sunday none of the directors was about and the idea was that I'd take it back later that night and nobody would be any the wiser. So, everyone piled into the back of the firm's van and we set off for Southport.

I parked up on some waste ground; we all went into the nearest chippy – fish, chips and mushy peas all round – and we were off for the day. When we got back at about 12 at night, the van had gone. So there I am, stranded, with all these girls. The language was absolutely choice, I can tell you! I had no alternative but to go and find the nearest police station and report it. I told them, 'You won't miss it, it's got Edwin Butterworth's in big letters all over it.'

We had to make our own way back to Manchester on the train and God knows how or what time it was in the end, but we finally managed it. The police found the van a few days later parked on a little country lane in the middle of nowhere on the outskirts of Southport. In the back were two little piglets! Apparently, there'd been a spate of pig and sheep stealing ('rustling' I think the cowboys call it) in the area and the police thought it was these thieves who'd stolen our van.

It was amazing, really, looking back, that when I explained the theft to the management at Butterworth's, they just let me off. I told them what had happened, all about the day out for the girls and the flat tyres and everything, and they basically said, 'Don't worry about it.' I'm sure it was only the fact that they liked me so much that I got away with it.

Nowadays, the least anyone would expect in a similar situation would be the sack.

Despite my little unauthorised excursion with the van, as I got on at Butterworth's, the time came when I was given a company car. Ironically enough, it was the exact same one the manager, Mr Desmond, used to have. See – I told you I was going to get a big car! I'd been to a meeting one day with David Stansfield and was driving him back to work when we stopped at some traffic lights on Ashton New Road – right outside Bowers' Pawn Shop. I had a quick glance and saw loads of clothes hanging up in the window and on racks outside. One jacket in particular caught my eye and I turned to my passenger. I said, 'David, do you see that jacket? The one on the "forfeited pledge" rail. The one for sale for 17 shillings.'

He said, 'Yes, what about it?'

'It's mine,' I said.

He laughed at first and didn't believe me. I told him honestly that it was one my mum had taken in a long time ago and, as I'd since gone up in the world, she hadn't bothered to go and get it back.

It was while I was at Butterworth's that I had my one and only 'proper' date with a girl. I thought I'd do it for bravery. Her name was Stella Kershaw and she worked in the offices at Butterworth's. On the evening of the date, I'd arranged to pick her up but we were two drivers short at work and so, at the last minute, I was roped into driving an articulated lorry fully loaded with 15 tons of waste paper. I dropped the load off and then drove into town – in the lorry and still dressed in my overalls – and met her outside the Grand Hotel on Aytoun Street.

She was standing on the corner with her little handbag on her arm and I shouted to her, 'Come on, get in. I've got to clock out.' It wasn't the most romantic of moments. Stella was a nice girl and the date went well but I think the only reason I fancied her in the first place was that she was a tall girl and I wanted to get into her frocks!

Stella was from the Bradford district of Manchester and her mother used to run an outdoor beer licence on the corner of Mill Street. I'd first met my date back at school and we used to do a bit of dancing together at the school socials. For the night out we went to the pictures, the Don, at the bottom of Ashton New Road. We went to see the musical *Oklahoma!*. We could only afford one ice cream so we shared a tub with a little spoon but there was none of this sitting on the back row business. At one point, I did put my arm around her but then I thought Oh no, I can't be doing with this, and anyway she was bigger than me and I thought she should have been her putting her arm around me!

Another chap who worked in the office had the wonderful name of Terry Maffia. Who could forget a name like that? We had a lot of fun together – I think he was on the same wavelength as me – and the pair of us would often waltz around the office together without a care in the world. I don't think it came as any kind of surprise to Terry when I finally made it as *Foo Foo*. He knew as well as I did that, although Butterworth's employed me and paid the bills, showbiz was my true love.

I can also remember someone I suppose would have been called 'the office junior', a young man by the name of Robin

Strickland. I believe Robin is nowadays still in the same line of business and a happily married family man, but back then he had the privilege to work under me ... so to speak. He was a smashing lad and I knew he was destined to go a long way in the company; in fact, I think he was still there when the factory finally closed some time in the 1980s.

As well as progressing in the company, I was also making progress in the showbiz world. Even though I had by now become quite popular and in reasonable demand on the club circuit, to me it was still a bit of fun and I never really expected to make it that big. And then I got for me – at least – what I considered to be a big break. I played the Princess Sporting Club on Grey Mare Lane in Beswick, although to me it could well have been the London Palladium. I turned up for the booking in my Ellis's meat pie van and none other than the late, great Les Dawson was also on the bill. To be truthful, I can't remember the exact date but it must have been the late 1950s and it was the beginning of a terrific friendship that lasted until Les's tragic death in 1993. Like me, Les, too, was born in Manchester (in his case, also a working-class district, this time Collyhurst) and was trying to make it as a stand-up comic, a very difficult task in the notoriously difficult working-men's clubs of the north of England. When he won *Opportunity Knocks* on television in 1967, the country finally saw what a wonderful talent he had, something that we in the club scene had known for years.

Les asked me what time I was due on stage and went on to say that he had another gig on the same night, this one at the Northern Sporting Club on Rochdale Road in Harpurhey, a place run by Dougie Flood (who later owned Bredbury Hall) and Geoff Reeves. I said that I was on at 8.00pm, had just the one gig that night and, as I also had the luxury of transport (admittedly, just the van, although it did impress Les as he still went everywhere on the bus), I'd wait for him and run him up to the next show. So I did my spot – five songs – and then, as promised, waited for Les and we set off for Harpurhey. The Northern Sporting Club was a lovely place to play with a super stage, and as Les was waiting to go on, no less than Tommy Cannon and Bobby Ball (know then as The Harper Brothers) were coming off. I liked the look of this new style of venue and, indeed, the circuit it appeared to be part of, and I asked Les how he got to be so involved with it. He simply told me to ring these people up and tell them what I'd done and where I'd played, finishing with the memorable, 'You've got to push yourself.'

Recalling that story about Les Dawson and my van reminds me of another. It was a similar scenario; Les had asked me to give him a lift to a show we were both appearing in, which I gladly did, only this time when we came out of the venue, the van was gone. We both stood there for a minute trying to remember if I'd parked it somewhere else, until we finally realised that the van had been stolen. As we had no money between us, we had no other option but to walk home. I reported the theft to the police and, a few days later, they got in touch to tell me they'd found it. It was in perfect order, no damage at all and was full of petrol. Also, in the back were two brand-new wireless sets. I don't think the police ever found anyone (neither did they question the wirelesses), but I think someone had stolen the van simply to carry out a robbery on a television and radio shop somewhere. The full tank of petrol and the wireless sets were just their way of saying thank you. Needless to say, the petrol was very well received and I sold the wireless sets for £8 each to a scrap-dealer.

Taking Les's advice on board from the Northern Sporting Club, I began to 'ring these people up'. One of the people I rang was Renee Rhythm – or, as she was known affectionately, 'Big Bouncing Renee' – who had the George and Dragon on Ashton Old Road. I'd been told to ring her by Tony Marsden who was a singer and compère at Renee's club, who'd said to me, 'You've got to come and sing at Renee's.'

'Will I get paid for it?' I asked, and his reply was straight to the point.

'Well, if you do it once and she likes you, then yes.'

So I went, sang, she liked me and I got paid.

Renee was a real character and looked a lot like a bigger version of Dame Edna Everage, even down to the huge glasses with diamantes. Renee was the first thing you'd see when you went into the club. She had her own table right next to the door and was always to be found sitting there with a drink in one hand and a white fluffy poodle – complete with diamante collar – perched on her knee. She looked like a Buddha in drag! Back then I used to sing a bit of everything, really, whether it was the older, big-band, crooner-style of song or whatever was currently the flavour of the month. I did quite a few charity shows at Renee's as time went on, with admission in the region of 2s every time!

Throughout this time, at all those clubs and pubs, I was still Frank Pearson. Occasionally a bit camp, admittedly, but no mention, signs or even thoughts of Foo Foo. All that was to change, however, when I was asked back to Lawson's Cotton Mill for another staff Christmas party.

3

Foo Foo Lammar... Beginners Please

*T*O THIS DAY, I still don't know how it all came about, but two of the girls I used to work with at Lawson's, Iris Young and Sylvia Wren, said to me, 'You've got to put the wig on.'

'What wig?' I replied.

Then they produced this red curly wig, one that they'd bought from the front at Blackpool on a works' outing. 'We've got a frock as well and we'll get you made up – go on, it's Christmas,' they went on.

'All right then,' I agreed, and the girls got to work on me. Another of the girls, Iris Stone, had ordered some white stiletto shoes from a catalogue and they also produced this long white frock complete with fringes. I was all set to go on stage when Iris said, 'Wait a minute; you can't go on as Frank looking like that. What are we going to call you?'

One of the big Hollywood stars back then was Hedy Lamarr, and there'd been a feature on her recently in a magazine. Not that we bought magazines, but we saw (and read) literally hundreds of them when they became waste paper. She was well known for all the glamour and wigs, so Iris suggested they announced me as Miss Hedy Lamarr. The compère for the show was an overseer (or foreman) at the factory; he'd had a bit of experience himself working the clubs (he'd been a pantomime dame, if memory serves) and also happened to be French. I think he was a bit gay as well, but it takes all sorts and to each his own as I always say. His name was Jacques someone or other, and he came up with the name '*Foo Foo*'. I don't know where he got it from – maybe he'd been to the Follies in Paris – but the name sounded just right and so I did my first show as Miss Foo Foo Lammar, with a slight alteration to the spelling. The date was Christmas 1964. I sang about five or six songs (one of which was 'There Is Nothing Like a Dame') and remember really camping it up with that frock on, although the shoes were a different matter. I could hardly walk in the bloody things they were so high. The name Foo Foo stuck with me even after the show and, as time progressed, more and more people began to call me by it.

I loved the reception and recognition I got after the show from all the staff in that canteen. Wearing the wig and the frock (but not necessarily those particular shoes) and camping it up even more than usual gave me a huge thrill, and I thought to myself, I'll have some more of this.

I started to go to the Cheshire Cheese, a pub at the bottom of Oldham Road close to the old *Daily Express* building. Rudi

Mancini, a local Italian musician, ran it and he'd often put on drag shows with Diamond Lil topping the bill. I can remember Lil's language was awful; every other utterance was the 'F' word. Some even said (although I never actually saw it) that she kept a cut-throat razor concealed down the back of her dress for particularly rough audiences. Even though all these acts were a lot older than me, I used to watch fascinated and tried to pick up some pointers for my own newly discovered act. I soon found out that Foo's wardrobe would have to be improved. In her very early days (I can remember wearing this outfit at the Devonshire Music Hall) I used to have a pair of huge shoes that made me look as though I had club feet and was poured into a dress that must have been at least 12 sizes too small. To top it all off was a big curly wig. I looked like a brillo pad on heat! But the fact that I was a little light on the top-quality clothes did not prevent me from going to the occasional show on the bus. I wasn't bothered by any strange looks or comments I received; indeed, it gave me an opportunity to catch a glimpse of what other women wore on their nights out. There were one or two people, though, who thought they'd have a laugh at my expense. On more than one occasion I'd turn up (in full drag) at a pub or club for some charity do or other, only to be told that they knew nothing about me or this supposed show and that I'd been stitched up. Oh well – tiny things for tiny minds ...

Another drag act who appeared regularly at the Devonshire was Bunny Lewis. He used to put on his own shows there and one had the lovely title of *Soldiers In Skirts*. I knew Bunny fairly well but he tended to mix with just a small number of the same people – other drag acts mainly – and the whole group was a bit 'cliquey'. That was his decision and I respected him for it, but I never wanted to be a part of that scene. I also didn't want to be stamped 'a silly drag queen'. I know that we are, of course, called that by some but, in my eyes, I see myself as an entertainer. I've always been able to entertain an audience with or without a frock. If a law was introduced tomorrow saying that it was illegal for men to wear women's clothes, then it wouldn't bother me in the slightest. I know I could still make a living. Thank God that I can look just as good in either!

Not too long after that Christmas show, I went for a day trip to Blackpool on a charabanc (we called it a 'sharra') from the Ardwick Empire on the green. Remembering this trip, from this great old Manchester landmark, also brings back more memories of my dad. When he'd finally had enough of rag and boning, he went into the demolition business and one of the buildings he worked on was the Ardwick Hippodrome, another fine Manchester theatre and one that used to stand on the other side of the roundabout from the Empire. One particular day, while working at the Hippodrome, he had a really bad accident when a steel girder fell on him and split his head open. He was taken to Manchester Royal Infirmary and was on the danger list for months. We were told that, even if he survived, he might never be fit enough to work again. As I said earlier, Dad was a big, strong fella and I'm sure it was this strength that finally got him through in the end, although the damage was so severe he was still very ill and was never really the same man again after the accident.

Not too far from the Don Cinema (the scene of my one and

only female date) was the Ancoats Arms, on Ancoats Lane, another Manchester pub I performed in. I did a lunchtime charity show there one day to try and raise money for some poor soul who'd been knocked down and badly injured by a taxi. I got changed and put my make-up on during a break at Butterworth's and then drove round to the pub. I did the show (with my good friend of many years, compère Rusty King) dressed as Foo Foo – this time slightly differently. I took the frock off and underneath I wore nothing but a bathing suit, stilettos and wig, and was stretched full length across the piano singing 'All of Me' when I saw these three burly blokes standing in the doorway watching me. These three were very noticeable because the rest of the pub seemed to be full of old women. Another thing I noticed was the hair of the man standing in the middle. It was very curly and belonged to my dad! He'd just finished a weighing and had called in with a couple of his mates for a pint on his way home.

He didn't even know about Foo, and when he saw me lying there on top of that piano I could well imagine what he was thinking. I didn't have to imagine what came next – I can still see it now! I saw this thing flying towards me and it wasn't until my tits went one way, my wig went the other and I was flat on the floor – with one leg still inside the piano lid – that I knew. He'd picked up a stool and hurled it at me from almost the full length of the pub. I can still hear his astonished words as well – 'That's my currant bun up there – with a bleedin' frock on!'

I was absolutely terrified of what he might do next, so I picked up all my belongings as quickly as I could and, fortunately for me as it was a scorching summer's day, the fire exit door was open, and I literally flew through it. I got back to Butterworth's and retold the story to all the girls who, of course, thought it was hilarious.

I, on the other hand, was terrified of what my dad might do to me when I got home that night. I couldn't dare go home so I managed to get a message to my brother Tommy to tell Mum I was all right, but would be spending the next few nights at my gran's. I understood fully Dad's reaction; after all, it wasn't as though there were as many drags acts then as there are today. Of course, nowadays the Manchester Village is full of them but, back then, there were hardly any to speak of so the majority of ordinary people didn't know what they were.

The other thing, of course to take into account is my upbringing. The last thing he would have contemplated was seeing his eldest son dressed as a woman. It must have been quite a shock for Dad to witness such a stark contrast to what he thought I was growing up to be and the way I actually was.

He used to love my singing as a teenager and would regularly encourage me to 'Get up and give 'em a song, son,' whenever we found ourselves in the same pub. He had hands like shovels and could just pick me up easily and plonk me on a stool in front of everyone. I'd often seen him walk round with a hat prising a few coppers from folk for the young singer trying to make his way. The same number of times I'd think to myself, Where's that bloody money gone? Each time I knew; Dad would have a few more pints with it.

But, like most things, time heals, and Dad never mentioned the piano and the stool to me again right up until the day he died. I don't know whether or not he approved of what I was doing but in the end he seemed to accept it and the incident in the Ancoats Arms just passed into history.

Even though I didn't know it at the time, I suppose that one incident was the start of my comedy career. At the time, although both my dad and me didn't think it was in the least bit funny, I'm sure everyone else in the pub (and even me now looking back) thought it was highly comical. Another thing that would have made it still funnier was my appearance. Nowadays, of course, it's not unusual for me to spend 'a few bob' on make-up, frocks and wigs, but in those days I had to make do with what I could borrow and I've no doubt I must have looked like Worzel Gummidge's mother.

* * *

Because I'd got on well at Butterworth's and was at the time on my way to becoming a junior director, I arranged for Dad to get a job as assistant to Pat Henshaw, a bloke who collected the waste paper for us in his lorry. I always gave Pat extra work so he, in turn, could manage to find a few extra bob to pay Dad.

I knew that I could continue my career at a higher level at Butterworth's apart from one small thing – I liked to put the frocks on too much! All the staff there knew what they could and couldn't get away with with me. They could try and kid the directors, whereas I was a different kettle of fish. I was one of them; I'd started from the bottom and knew all the shortcuts. It's difficult to measure any improvements I made in purely financial terms. I always describe it as me being 'the one on the cattle drive who got the most cattle through', and that includes both the girls and the drivers. Another promotion made me the transport manager and I'd think nothing of getting in my car and following a 20-ton articulated truck around the streets checking on what the driver was doing and where he was going. It was not unknown for them to complete their log-books with stories such as 'held up at such and such a place for an hour because of traffic'. I didn't stand for any of that; I knew when they were skiving. Once they knew I was on to their little schemes, it tightened things up a lot which, in turn, benefited the company.

I was eventually promoted to the board at Butterworth's, but this also led to the end of my 'wearing my beret to work' days. And just as I did during my brief flirtation with the Army, I still liked to use pipe cleaners in my hair; mind you, they were only used to enhance what natural curls I already had, you understand. Thursdays and Fridays were the most popular beret-wearing days at Butterworth's, because it meant that if I had a show on at night, my hair was very nearly ready by the time I got home from work. I attended one particular board meeting the day after I'd had my hair streaked once, and sat there wearing a flat cap. One of the directors noticed this and commented, 'Mr Pearson, you look a little different today.'

'Yes, I've been baling and all the lime from the bags keeps getting in my hair,' I said.

He accepted my excuse, but it was a complete lie; I still had my curlers in underneath!

If things were going well at work, they were also going well for me on the showbiz scene. With lots of regular bookings, I was now earning up to £30 a night in the pubs and, because I was still living with my gran, I'd managed to put a bit away here and there. Just around the corner from Gran's, on Wilson Street, a two-up, two-down house came up for sale at £160 and I bought it, for cash, from the estate agent. I paid for it all to be decorated and furnished (even with a television) and moved Mum and Dad in together. Dad had received £5,000 compensation from his accident, and it was obvious from seeing them together that they were very happy living in that little house.

Even though Dad was nowhere near the man he was, he stuck at that job with Pat for about five years until, one day, I got a phonecall from Pat while I was at Butterworth's. Pat was working with Dad collecting waste paper from a bank in Altrincham. He walked round the back of the van with a load only to find Dad lying on the floor dead. It was June 1969; Dad was 54. The doctors said he'd had a heart-attack, but I knew it was the effects of the accident that had finally caught up with him.

I remember vividly the day being hot and sunny as I left work and drove up to see Mum and tell her the awful news. I also remember the chicken salad that she'd already prepared and laid out on the kitchen table ready for Dad's tea when he came home. We went to see Dad at the hospital and Mum was absolutely devastated by the news. Dad knew he'd done wrong previously and really tried hard to make it up to Mum at the end. Even though they'd had their problems and difficulties in the past, the last four or five years, in that little house on

Wilson Street, had been very happy ones and they still loved each other.

Dad was always full of fun and would call Mum by her full name, Leah Winifred, adding 'from the land of the flying piss-pots', an affectionate name for the Jersey Street dwellings she was brought up in. Mum had a difficult time coming to terms with his death, and his funeral at Gorton Cemetery was probably the hardest time of all, although, because of her strength of character, she managed to pull through in the end.

* * *

Even though I had a good job at Butterworth's, by now I'd built up a good reputation around the pubs and clubs and, in all honesty, the only thing that interested me was the singing. I had this new character in my life – Foo Foo – I was earning a good salary (along with a bit of fiddle) and had a company car, and yet, I still wasn't happy. I wasn't satisfied; I wanted more.

It was at this time that I went back to the Robin Hood on London Road, one of my earlier haunts. Eric Pearson the pianist was still there and I became a regular feature, performing anything up to four nights a week. I don't really know why I went back but, at the time, it felt like the right thing to do. Foo Foo came with me. In fact, she began almost to take over my act completely. The pub attracted a real mixture of people, both straight and gay, but at the time I didn't know where I fitted in really, so to me they were just people.

One regular in the pub was a gentleman by the name of

John. I never knew his second name and to this day still don't. I just knew him as 'old John'. He was a very smart man, quite a bit older than me, always well turned out, drank nothing more than half a mild and was extremely well spoken. I don't know whether he looked on me as a sort of son (or a daughter even), whether he was gay or whatever, but he took a shine to me and started to give me a bit of money and buy me little gifts. I think he saw me as a lovely, 'vagabond' lad. By vagabond I mean I lived life to the full, I enjoyed myself and enjoyed making other people enjoy themselves. I remember one particular birthday when he bought me a beige Crombie overcoat and a beautiful gold watch. I didn't even know what a Crombie was and, as for gold, well, it was a thing I'd heard about but had certainly never seen. Apart from keeping good time, that watch also helped with the family finances. It had a good few trips backwards and forwards from the pawn shop.

I never saw John outside the pub; I didn't know where he lived, and I didn't know anything about his family; in fact, the only thing I knew for certain about him was that he came from money. His appearance, grooming and manners confirmed this. He would chat to me regularly in the pub and simply said, 'Go on, make me laugh.' Well, being a bit cocky and something of a character even back then, I tried my best and he seemed to enjoy himself – sometimes I saw tears of laughter rolling down his cheeks – and so everyone was happy. I used to sing songs for him; one of his particular favourites was 'You'll Never Know Just How Much I Love You'. I think this used to bring back happy family memories for him. I got the impression that, although he was undoubtedly wealthy, he hadn't had much laughter and happiness in his life. Without being too pompous, when I look at the way Sarah Ferguson was with Prince Andrew, it reminds me of the way I was with John. Fergie gave a new lease of life to Andrew. She was a commoner (although not quite as common as me!) who not only made him laugh, but also made him do things up until then he'd never have dreamt of doing as a member of the Royal Family. It was a bit like that for John and me.

Not long after receiving my birthday presents, John was chatting to me about his forthcoming holiday (to Cornwall to see his sister) and asked me where I was going for my summer holidays. I explained that what with the uncertainty of things at home, I had not really thought about it, let alone booked anywhere. Come to think of it, I'd never even had a holiday up to then. I said I'd seen pictures of the Isle of Man, with the three legs and the boat and everything, and that it looked very nice. John said that there were some lovely bars on the island and that I'd have a great time. He didn't like the idea of the boat, though. He suggested flying. Well, that was it as far as I was concerned. Flying anywhere was still for the super-rich in those days.

In the end, John paid for me, Mum, Gran and my youngest brother Brian to fly to the Isle of Man and stay for a week in a boarding house. None of us could believe it; it was a fantastic gesture and I never knew how much the whole thing cost. We stayed at Douglas Head, right on the front and had a lovely time. Not far from the boarding house was the Douglas, a huge pub and one we'd see every day as we came and went. One day, I saw a sign going up in the pub window. It read

'Talent Night Tonight – £100 First Prize'. Because I was on holiday, I didn't have Foo's outfit with me but I thought, Well, as I'm here, I might as well have a go.

So I went in at lunchtime and had a beef and onion sandwich (why do I remember what I had to eat?) and told them I wanted to put my name down for the talent show. That night, I went back and found myself pitted against nine other acts. These included an accordionist and an 'experienced' male and female comedy duo called Rough and Ready. So, in front of a pub full of holidaymakers out for a good time, I did my bit and managed to come away with the first prize of £100. Not only would the £100 come in very handy for the holiday, but I was also told that I'd actually just won one of a series of heats and the final was to be held in four weeks' time. Unfortunately, by then I would be back in Manchester and so I had to turn down the offer.

Later, when my twenty-first birthday came round, Mum and the family were arranging (as best they could) a little buffet for me at the Lord Napier on Grey Mare Lane. When John found out about this, he immediately (and unbeknown to me) sent some money to the pub and soon a little party turned into a big one. I can remember seeing for the first time proper, thick slices of ham on the sandwiches and *real* meat pies. Strangely enough, though, he didn't turn up on the night. I most certainly did, dressed in my splendid new overcoat and watch; I must have looked like a member of the mafia! I saw John a few times afterwards and thanked him again for his generosity but, as time went on and I began to progress in showbiz, we gradually lost touch.

Sometimes even today, I still think back and wonder just what happened to him.

That win on the Isle of Man along with the death of my father made me even more determined to make a go of it in showbusiness. Even though I say so myself, I did a good job for Butterworth's and the directors loved me for it. Although they didn't know about Foo, they knew I had a singing interest outside my 'proper' job. What they didn't realise was just how strongly I felt about it and how determined I was to succeed. I felt so passionate about becoming a household name that my job, my car and anything else I had of value at that time took second place to becoming a star. So at the age of 21, young, talented and good-looking (so good-looking that I fancied myself!), I renewed my plan to become famous and have my name up in lights.

Outside the major clubs and cabaret venues, however, because of my status within showbusiness at the time, various charities such as The Blind Association, Cancer Research and many other local causes were calling upon my time, and though the charity work slowed me down on my way to stardom, I believed then, as I do today, that there are many people worse off than myself and I was determined to do all I could to help the various organisations that asked me to help raise money for them.

One particular charity event called upon me to open a jumble sale at a local church hall in Stockport. There was an eager crowd awaiting Frank Lammar and the grand opening, and after my usual honest and vulgar address to the waiting throng, I cut the piece of red ribbon that was across the doorway of the church hall. Inside the hall, hung up on one of the stalls which was selling second-hand clothing of all types was a blue and silver sequinned dress, size fourteen and, though I'd never been in a frock professionally, the idea was obviously in the back of my head. The gown was the princely sum of six pounds, and I just *had* to have it.

Some months after the purchase, I was invited to a fancy dress old-time music hall to raise funds for an old-age pensioners Christmas party, which prompted the appearance of my jumble sale gown. To complete my look, I borrowed a blonde Vera Duckworth wig from a lady who had undergone chemotherapy but no longer needed it. I arrived at the venue complete with a carrier bag containing my wardrobe: gown, wig and high-heeled shoes. The landlady showed me to the star dressing room – the toilet – and within this humble room the transformation took place. Duly ready, I was introduced on stage where my orchestra awaited: a 79-year-old pianist who I had never met before – he must have been one of the old-age pensioners! I had been on stage ten minutes when a middle-aged woman shouted, 'That's my frock, I gave that to a jumble sale.' The frock was more famous than me – I nearly died of shame. That was the first and last appearance of the gown! I wasn't ready to wear a frock on stage, especially somebody else's.

The day job was keeping me busy, bailing seven hundredweight of waste paper on a huge press with my four female assistants. Those girls had bigger muscles than I could ever have. One girl, Sylvia, was a real character. She was fourteen stone and covered in so many tattoos that her body looked like a roll of heavily-patterned wallpaper. She gave me lots of material for the act, although she never knew it. In fact most of my act back then consisted of material picked up from the women I worked with as the department had 65 women and one man ... ME! With a background like that is it any wonder I never married!

One night, Sylvia took me out with colleagues to the Cheshire Cheese. As we went through the door, we were greeted by very loud, but very good, music. On stage was 'Diamond Lil' and her sidekick, Neville Sinclair, another drag queen with a beautiful soprano voice. I found out later that the organist accompanying them was Rudi Mancini. We all enjoyed the night and ended up in an Indian curry house. Unknown to my Butterworth's workmates, I went back to that pub on several occasions, mainly because I thought the organist was brilliant and I wanted to have that man behind me (on backing of course!). On one occasion I got on stage and performed. The audience loved me; the two drag queens hated me. Diamond Lil had said to Rudi, 'If that man gets up again and takes over the show, WE LEAVE!' To my amazement, Rudi said, 'This is my pub; it's a nice change for the punters to be entertained without the drag.' They didn't leave! I carried on using Rudi's talented backing to enhance the musical side of my act, but still in my heart I was aiming for bigger and better things.

It was around this time that I first met a very talented woman called Lynne Perrie, who later went on to play the part of Ivy Tilsley in *Coronation Street*, and who at this time was doing the rounds of the local pub and club circuit and had the most beautiful singing voice I had ever heard. I was the support act to her at one show at a rugby club and after the show Lynne and I became friendly and got really pissed together. Her voice and status made me all the more determined to get to the top – it was a pleasure to see her perform, and I wanted people to see me work and have the same feeling about my show. I felt I was actually starting to work with the right types of acts and that I was beginning to climb further up the all-important billing ladder.

I can remember being asked to take part in an all-star football match for a charity in aid of disabled children, along with the likes of former *Coronation Street* star Chris Quentin, Bernard Manning, The Harper Brothers (who found fame and hit the big time as Cannon and Ball) and Les Dawson. It was us celebs versus doctors, nurses and other medical staff. It was a fun day and my role was that of First Aider and part-time goalie on our team. If there was an injury, it was my job to revive the patient. Needless to say, nobody admitted to needing treatment, they were either a brave bunch or terrified of what I had to offer in the way of First Aid! Mind you, all there was in my First Aid case was a large jar of Vaseline, some plasters and a wire brush!

The whole day's effort raised several thousand pounds, which was a lot of money at the time and the thought of my First Aid raised a few blood pressures as well! The final score: Celebs six, Doctors, etc. – who obviously fiddled – eight! It's a good job we weren't playing a team of accountants!

This football match also attracted the attention of the press, which of course was good news for my career. And of course, now I was working with and meeting higher profile acts, Frank Lammar was beginning to work and associate with nationally-known names.

Some months later, as a result of the press coverage, I was approached by an amateur ladies' netball team from Manchester, who raised money for various charities. They asked if I would join the team as their medic after seeing the report in the papers of the celebrity football match. I joined the team, keeping the same lucky medical bag complete with wire brush, etc.! During my reign I saw more tits and teeth on match days than a plastic surgeon with a half share in a dental practice!

Ironically, years later two musicians who knew of my involvement with the netball team wrote a song for me entitled 'Foo Foo's Netball Team' which was released on the EMI Record label. Unfortunately, although it was very well received, I couldn't leave Manchester at the time to go off around the country to promote the single, which was a shame because EMI were so pleased with the reaction to the single that they wanted me to release an album of the same name, which again involved too much time in London. I had to say no. For the time being that was the end of my aspirations to be a pop idol.

One night, I was doing my show at a pub called the Salisbury, which was opposite the gates at Salford docks. In the audience was a group of British sailors with their boss, the chief petty officer. I gave them a good laugh by taking the piss out of him for most of the show. He actually loved it and after the show invited me to an open day on board his submarine (well, Her Majesty's), HMS *Manchester*, the following day. Well! How could I refuse a boat full of seamen! My passion came out like a painter's blow lamp. I got the full VIP tour. I visited every cabin on the whole boat; I visited everyone from top to bottom! I nearly got dragged up on deck to offer my services as a cleaner free of charge. God alone knows what would have happened if I'd only thought to bring my trusty wire brush along on that gig!

As time went by, my performances and stunts got more outrageous and my popularity as a character grew fast. At this time, though, I didn't know whether I was Arthur or Martha and I was just as camp as a row of tents! But, within the pub and club scene, the name of Frank Lammar was growing and so was the act and my experience, both on and off the stage. The more I worked, the more the name of Frank Lammar guaranteed a full house at any venue. My career was taking off!

* * *

It must have been around this time that I tried to help my brother Tommy with his coal business. I say help but, in all honesty, I was neither use nor ornament. Tommy was doing quite well at the time, having made the transformation from working down the pit in Bradford to running his own fuel company in Marple with about four or five lorries. You must remember that a lot of people still had coal fires back then, and it wasn't too unusual to see Pearson's Coal wagons trundling through the streets of Manchester. Nowadays, he takes a backseat to the everyday running of his business, leaving it in the hands of his two sons David and Anthony and his grandson Darren.

I remember the day in question because it was a Saturday. I wasn't due to go to work at Butterworth's, so I had the day off before doing a show that night. Tommy had recently had to let his other helper go when the dole found out he was working but still claiming benefit. Because of this, he was a man short and so roped me in to help him.

Tommy used to go to the coal yard where he'd fill the sacks prior to loading on to his lorries and then he'd be off on his rounds. But, before loading, each sack would have to be weighed just in case he got a visit from the Weights and Measures man. Well, we got down to the yard and when I saw these sacks I told him straight, 'I can't be lifting those things.'

He replied bluntly, 'Oh, get on the bleedin' truck. I'll lift 'em up, you just stack 'em neatly.'

Eventually, we got the wagon loaded but I really struggled trying to handle these sacks and the bloody coal kept falling out and going all over the place. I just left all this loose stuff on the floor of the wagon because, obviously, now the sacks were lighter they were much easier to move around and stack. We were about an hour into the round when Tommy got pulled over – by the Weights and Measures man. Not surprisingly, most of the sacks were half-empty by now and therefore well under the required weight.

Desperately, I tried to pick up these pieces of coal and refill the sacks but the Weights and Measures man was not interested. How I wish the television cameras could have been there to record that moment. For some reason, I'd gone to help Tommy wearing white jeans which in itself was bad enough, but so concerned was I with not damaging my nails, I had a pair of gloves on as well. I can still see me clearly holding out individual lumps of coal between my gloved thumb and forefinger and gingerly (so to speak) dropping them one at a time into these sacks.

It took me about three hours to pick up every last piece of coal and then, just to make matters worse, Tommy refused to pay me a penny for my efforts. Mind you, I can't blame him; I did make a right town halls of it. That was the end of my career as a coalman; surprisingly, Tommy never asked me to help him again.

* * *

Whilst driving home from work one night in 1971, I picked up a copy of the *Manchester Evening News*. After checking to see if I was in it (I wasn't – again!), for no particular reason I began to look through the 'for sale' pages. Amongst all the hundreds of others, one ad caught my eye. It read: 'Nightclub for sale – Central Manchester – Shudehill –The Picador Club – owing to loss of licence.' So I circled the ad, rang them up and made an appointment to go and see it. The owner at the time, Georgie Derbyshire, wanted £6,700 for the lease.

When I first entered the place, it had been standing empty for a few months. It just looked as though everyone had left things as they were, gone home and never come back. Knives, forks and plates were still on the tables and the floors hadn't seen a Hoover or mop bucket in ages. The leftover food had brought with it the inevitable consequence – mice. Absolutely bloody hundreds of them. They were leaping from table to table, scurrying under foot, jumping out of boxes – everywhere you looked there were mice. It wasn't a pretty sight.

It was a two-floor club and, even though it was obviously in need of considerable repair, I began to visualise it the way I wanted it. Downstairs I saw a little cabaret room with a piano and me singing at the side of it and upstairs, for those who liked to dance, I saw a disco, or 'mixed grill' as it became known later. Even though I was a nobody, I knew immediately I wanted the place. I felt this was my beginning. The only problem now was the money. Although I was not as close to the breadline as I had been in the past, I worked out, that if I did this, sold that and took everything into account, I could scrape together a maximum of £600. You don't have to be Einstein to work out that I was just a little bit short of the asking price!

Fortunately, fate was on my side at just the right moment in the shape of Brian Lucas. Brian was in both the scrap and construction businesses (we'd actually crossed paths in business at Butterworth's) and, along with his wife Brenda, had seen me perform many times at different venues around Manchester. I told Brian I'd seen a club I'd love to buy and he immediately said, 'OK, I'll come in with you.'

The next day, I went to the bank (Barclays on Ashton New Road) where fortunately they both knew and trusted me and they lent me my half of the money. Brian put up the other half and we were in business.

Mum was a bit sceptical at first about me going into business on my own. Perhaps, not surprisingly, she saw it as a risk and saw me as someone who entertained on a part-time basis from the stage as opposed to someone who was responsible full-time for not only the building, but also everything that goes with it. Although she knew deep down how much I wanted it, I'm sure the thought of me giving up a good job (which undoubtedly I had at Butterworth's) was also nagging away at the back of her mind. I'm also sure Mum was no different to any other mother in that respect.

I got all my brothers involved and between us we arranged to get rid of the mice, polished everything, cleaned the carpets, painted the toilets and even stuck down some of the old wallpaper. We did everything we could so we didn't have to buy anything new; we couldn't afford to. The club had a tiny sound system that was awful, so I got in touch with some friends from the club circuit and they helped out by letting me have a few 'bits and pieces'. I rang Eric Pearson, the pianist from the Robin Hood, offered him work along with Joe Lake, a drummer, and a lovely girl singer called Willa Forrest.

We opened the doors for the first time in November 1971. I'd been filling clubs and making money for other people for the best part of 20 years. Now it was time I started to make some for myself. It also meant that Foo Foo finally had a place to call her own. I left Butterworth's and became a 34-year-old, self-employed nightclub owner.

Like Mum, the management at Butterworth's were also concerned about what was undoubtedly a huge decision. They said to me, 'Look, keep the company car and have a couple of months off. Then, if things don't work out with the club, you can come back here.' Even though it was a lovely gesture, I was determined to make a go of it. I put my heart and soul into this new venture.

Well, at least most of my heart and soul went into it. Just in case things didn't work out at the club, I kept my hand in with the waste paper business. I bought an old pigsty (literally) in Failsworth, rang a few of my old contacts from Butterworth's and did a little bit of business on the side. Fortunately for me the club took off immediately and Pearson's Paper Mill in Failsworth was a very short-lived venture, but it did provide me with a safety net.

I did very little advertising as such (we didn't even change the name and kept the old Picador Club sign over the door) but I passed the word around through people I knew from the clubs, all the neighbours and friends of Mum's turned up and we were packed every night. Within 12 months of opening, I'd paid the bank back completely, bought a new Ford Zephyr (£800, I think it was) and had shoeboxes literally crammed full of money sliding around in its boot. We were open six, sometimes seven, nights a week and I never once took a day off. I couldn't afford to.

Looking back, I don't think I could have timed the opening any better. We got in right at the start of the glamorous Seventies just as the disco scene began and the whole thing just grew and grew and the money kept coming in. So much so, in fact, that I found myself in the fortunate (but still for me, strange) position of being able to buy a new house. Along with Alan Owen, I bought a bungalow for £4,600 on Alan Avenue in Failsworth, just off the posh Lord Lane estate and was, not surprisingly, very happy. Apart from one night when the house was burgled.

I decided I wanted to have some extra shelves put up and, through someone who worked at the club, I arranged for his friend to carry out the work. What I didn't know was that this other person had helped himself to a spare key and let himself in one night. It was around this time that I was taking some of the cash from the club home at nights and, looking back, I'm sure both Alan and myself were being watched and followed. At about 3.00 in the morning, Alan sat bolt upright in bed shouting, and there at the end of the bed stood a bloke about 6ft tall waving what looked like a bread knife above his head. When I realised I wasn't dreaming, I pretended I was on some kind of medication (mind you, I was in a daze) and began to feel under the bed for my non-existent pills. In fact, I was looking for a wooden stick I kept there for just such an incident. I never did find the bloody thing!

After the man had let his accomplice in from outside, they tied us up with our ties from the wardrobe and gagged us with the same socks we'd just been wearing. They then started to look for anything of value, and eventually they made off with some of my and Alan's jewellery and quite a bit of cash. Fortunately, Alan managed to untie himself and, still completely naked, ran next-door to get help and to call the police. The neighbour asked Alan, 'But where's Frank? How is he?' It was then the penny dropped for Alan; he'd left me still bound and gagged (and naked) in bed next-door!

A few weeks later, the thieves tried to sell one of my 'good' rings in a pub just around the corner from the bungalow. I think they only wanted £20 for it. Luckily, someone in the pub put two and two together and notified the police who eventually caught them. As they were also wanted for assaulting and robbing an old lady in the Post Office, they got ten years each for their trouble.

Back at the club, although it was successful, it was still hard work. Fortunately, I've got a terrific family and they all helped out right from the beginning. As for me, not only would I perform but I also worked behind the bar, in the cellar and, on nights when we were very short-staffed, I'd take my turn as the bouncer on the door alongside my brother Jimmy. I used to keep an old wooden arm from a dining room chair behind the entrance to the club for nights when things really got out of hand. I must have looked a picture dressed in a long evening dress and wig swinging this chair arm around my head for all I was worth! I got so carried away one night that I ended up (in full drag) kicking three real idiots down the stairs and out into the street. I got taken to court for that little incident. Ah, happy days.

One of the things we never seemed to get around to fixing at the club was the hole in the toilet floor. For ease of plumbing, when they'd put the toilets in they'd built the upstairs one directly above the downstairs one. The floor itself wasn't too clean at the best of times and the only thing stopping you from falling through to the downstairs toilet were a couple of beams. The worst thing about this hole, though, was its location, directly next to the toilet bowl itself. I've lost count of the number of times someone without full control has missed upstairs and the poor bloke downstairs was invariably covered in piss. What usually happened then was that the bloke downstairs rushed upstairs and a fight broke out. If we didn't have at least one fight a week because of these toilets we felt we'd got off lightly.

Things the public didn't see weren't that much better either. I can remember one night we decided we'd have a hot-pot supper for 200 paying customers. The only slight problem was that we didn't have any pans big enough to make the hot-pot in. So we improvised and used the next best thing. We took three fire buckets off the wall, emptied the sand and water out of them, got the mop bucket and painted all four of them a nice shade of cream and cooked the hot-pot in them. It was a bloody awful sight in the kitchen that afternoon. Even though we'd cleaned the buckets as best we could, when we cooked the potatoes, the boiling water brought all the remaining dirt to the surface and formed a horrible skin at the top. We had a lesbian working in the kitchen at the time called Scottie and I dressed her up in a white shirt and white hat so it would at least look like we had a proper chef. I also bought her a ladle and can remember the customers queuing *à la* school dinners in front of her whilst she slopped the hot-pot (it was more of a hotch potch than anything) out for them.

I did the show and watched as the audience tucked in and cleared their plates. When I'd finished I asked them if they enjoyed the food and went on to tell them that I'd bought the meat and potatoes myself from the cash and carry that morning and then cooked them that afternoon, *in three fire buckets and the mop bucket!* They didn't believe me at first, but when I brought two buckets out on stage to prove it – and showed them the bits left in the bottom – then they believed me!

Although I suppose that particular meal was at least partially successful, I will admit – and I know there are lots of people who'll agree with this – that I was not put on this earth to be a chef. When I was remembering the mop bucket fiasco, I also remembered another culinary occasion, this time with less successful results.

It occurred during the time at Foo Foo's when we opened for much of the day, from lunchtime until after the late-night show. We'd finished clearing away everything from lunchtime one day when, for some completely unknown reason, I said to Michael Ryan (a member of staff at the time who would later become my manager), 'Have you eaten yet?' When he said, 'No,' I told him, 'Right, get your coat. You're coming back to my house and I'll make us a bit of tea.'

Michael (who, with hindsight, now admits that he should have known better) was upstairs in the bedroom getting changed ready to go back to the club that evening as I put a meat pie in the oven. Once done, I then sat myself down in an armchair and before long had fallen into a deep sleep. I've no idea how long I was asleep but remember waking up when the cooker exploded! Unfortunately, there was no sign of what had been a lovely pie, so we went back to the club as hungry as we'd left it.

I don't think Michael had been with us long by then, but he proved to be a great help on more than the odd (and, believe me, there have been some very odd) occasions. In fact, he helped me out so much that I eventually took him on full-time and I've still got him today!

Someone else who helped me out a lot at the Picador was Colin Rigby, a long-standing friend who later became a business partner in Napoleon's. After working for several years in engineering with a company called Fletcher Millers, Colin was at the time running his own corrosion treatment business during the day and then spending his nights at the club helping me out with anything that needed doing. Don't ask me what his business involved; I didn't know back then and I still don't know now. Colin would accompany me on my regular trips to the cash and carry and the number of times we got caught trying to get away with only paying for half the goods was unbelievable! Fortunately, Colin is like me when it comes to the gift of the gab and somehow we always managed to talk ourselves out of it. Shocking, really, but it's a fact.

It wasn't unknown for us to have lots of dodgy drinks on the premises either. Buying them this way was obviously a lot cheaper (if not strictly legal) and we used to keep the illegal gin in empty R.White's Lemonade bottles. These we'd then mark with a large 'G' so as not to get them mixed up with the real lemonade. Somehow, the police found out about this and raided us. Unfortunately for them, one of their own had tipped us off in advance and in the end they found nothing. One of the reasons they never found anything was because the person who had tipped us off knew the places they were least likely to look and helped us to hide the stuff there! I can still see us all now passing the bottles up to others in the rafters.

Fortunately, at least as far as the club went, Colin was also more than capable of looking after himself. Before he went into engineering, he'd spent 12 years in the police force but

George & Dragon Hotel
5, Ashton Old Road
Thursday 15th Feb at 8 p.m.
A Grand Charity Concert
In Aid Of The Blind
Rusty King

PRESENTS ON STAGE

TONY MARSDEN   FRANK LAMMAR   ALAN HEYES
AVA   JACKIE NOLAN   TERRY NICHOLLS   RENNIE RYTHM

Donation 2/-

op: My old school, St Brigid's, the scene of my most embarrassing moment.

ottom: An early concert ticket – two shillings to see me!

Teddy Boy Pearson – 1962.

Top: Dinner at The Grand Hotel, Manchester, 1969, with amongst others Auntie Lorrie (Mum's sister), Alan Owen, me, my mum, Leah and her niece Joyce.

Bottom left and right: On the beach in Sitges, 1969. Have I no shame?

Taken in readiness for my appearance at The Great Room at London's Grosvenor House Hotel. The telephone number is for the Unit One sauna I used to own.

Top: Taken in The Picador Club in 1972. *Left to Right*: Mum's niece Joyce, Aunt Florrie, me on the mike, Mum, brother Tommy in the background and Tommy's wife, Shirley.

Bottom: With Tommy Doyle, more than twenty years after we lived behind the Prince of Wales.

Outside The Ranch Bar at Foo Foo's, mid 1970s.

On stage as Frank at Foo Foo's Palace in 1979.

Top: Meeting Princess Anne with Bonnie Langford.

Bottom: With Pete Waterman and his wife Denise.

reckons he had more fights at The Picador because of those toilets than he ever had as a policeman.

We had a regular clientele at the club and, although the majority of them were straight, we also attracted a few gays and lesbians. It was a good crowd who, on the whole (so to speak), tended to keep themselves to themselves, but I can honestly say there was never any trouble if and when they did meet.

The only time there was any real trouble was when we had the problems with the toilets. Sometimes, after a fight I'd get in such a state that I'd need a complete change of clothes, occasionally so much so that I had to go back home. I'd be in such a rush that it wasn't unknown for me to come back to the club wearing odd shoes. On one particular occasion, I was running so late that I came back wearing a spat!

The early part of the 1970s was a great time for me. The club was doing well; we had plenty of money coming in and we certainly weren't short of anything. Mum was in good health and enjoying herself and yet I still craved for one more thing. Call it an ego trip if you like, but I still wanted to be a name. I wanted to be a star. I wanted people to look around in the street and say, 'That's Foo Foo. That's Frank Lammar.' Even though I won Entertainer of the Year in 1973, at the time that just wasn't happening.

I won the northern heat of a national competition which was held at the Yew Tree pub in Wythenshawe, and I had to go to London for the final heat. This was held in somewhat grander surroundings – the Great Room at the Grosvenor House Hotel. Tickets for the night were £50 per head for dinner, a ten-act cabaret and stopover and 200 family, friends and fans from Manchester followed me down to London. Each of the ten acts was allowed a six-minute spot. I rehearsed in the afternoon and then, in the evening, I was given what I thought was the best position; I was on second from last so I knew more or less what I had to beat.

Before it was my turn to get up, I sat with Mum, my three brothers and their wives, friend and future business partner Colin Rigby and Dick and Marion Worley (landlord and landlady from the Prince of Wales) on one of the many round tables scattered around the room. I also had a few brandies, (quite a lot of brandies actually) and before I knew what had happened I was semi-pissed. It was the first time I had ever had a drink before a performance and it showed. When my turn came to get up on stage, I made a real balls of it.

As rehearsed, the orchestra brought me on with the opening theme from *Sunday Night at the London Palladium*. I greeted this by bursting into the song 'Mardi Gras', thinking I was still back at the Prince of Wales. I should have known then what was happening, but couldn't seem to stop myself.

I remember Charlie Chester was the compère for the evening and one of the judges was Wei Wei Wong, at the time a well-known personality, both as a dancer with The Young Generation and a familiar face on television quiz shows such as *Celebrity Squares*. I looked across at her and slurred, 'Hasn't she got a lovely face for a Jap.' Needless to say, the remark wasn't well received, neither was my comment to Petula Clark who was in the audience. 'She's got hair like a back-combed Weetabix,' I said about her. I also gave her a bit of pidgin

French such as "*zham buttee*" and the like to try and get a laugh, but it was hopeless.

In fact, I did everything apart from the act I'd rehearsed. I was far too gone and was simply daft (and rude) for the whole six minutes. Except, that is, for the few seconds when I fell off stage and landed in the floral arrangement! The organiser, Bernard Delfont, was less than impressed and, needless to say, I came nowhere in the end. The whole thing was undoubtedly my most embarrassing moment in showbiz. In fact, it was so awful, had it not been for the time when my trousers fell down during a school boxing match, it would have been the most embarrassing moment of my entire life. It certainly taught me a lesson, though, about drinking before a show and, to this day, I've never done it again.

I was angry with myself afterwards because – and I say this openly – I knew I could have easily beaten the other acts. I was also angry at the fact I'd let down those 200 people who'd spent all their hard-earned money travelling to London to support me. To top it all off, I had to stand brother Jimmy's bar bill for the evening as well! He thought his £50 ticket covered his drinks for the evening, and he kept ordering bottles of gin, vodka and all bloody sorts, thinking it was all in. When they measured the bottles at the end of the night Jimmy was completely pissed and so it was left to me to pay the bill.

Meanwhile back in Manchester, I loved The Picador Club and the opportunity it gave me but, deep down, I knew it was almost like a social club that was doing well. In fact, it was doing very well and made an awful lot of money. Some people might think that, because of my humble background, I would have been more than satisfied with the money and the trappings it gave me. But, deep down, I knew I wasn't going anywhere. After four years, I saw something that would give me the opportunity finally to get me what I wanted and, in the words of the Spice Girls, to take me where I wanted to go.

4

The King and Queen of Clubs

*I*N 1975, THE CELEBRITY Club on Dale Street, about half-a-mile or so from The Picador Club, came up for sale. It was run then by a man called Jack McCall with, I think, the help of some Greek money somewhere along the line. I'd heard that the club wasn't doing very well at the time and so I went to see Jack and told him I was interested in buying it. We agreed a price of £30,000 and so in I went. Although now he must be well into his eighties, Jack is still in the business; he owns The Press Club on Deansgate.

The Picador was a very posh club but I began to make changes almost immediately. It was too small for the kind of club I wanted. The first thing I did was to knock a wall down complete with statues that seemed to be taking the whole of the place up. It also contained The Ranch Bar, which, although not strictly part of the club itself, ran alongside. We used to have a speaker system rigged up at the time so that people in The Ranch Bar could still hear the show from the main room even if they couldn't see it. My old friend and fellow club owner Geoff Reeves was a regular in The Ranch Bar and I found out many, many years later that when he was in, he'd pull the plug on the speaker, so not only would he not see my act, the cheeky sod wouldn't hear it either! Mind you, he had heard it once or twice before! As soon as I'd finished, he'd plug it back in again and things would be back to normal. Later, when I went to see him to ask him how it went, he used to say things like, 'Oh, you were wonderful tonight, Frank,' knowing full well he hadn't heard a word of it.

I wasn't a name then and I knew I was taking a chance in what I was doing and so, just in case, I still kept The Picador and took on an old friend of mine, John Foster, as manager to run it for me. John would later come to work for me again, this time as manager of a sauna I was to buy.

As time went on, I began to show less and less interest in The Picador, until in the end, after about 12 months, I sold it and moved solely into The Celebrity, or Foo Foo's Palace as it had since been renamed. The new owners were my old pal Rusty King and Bunny Westley, a former Liverpool boxer who also owned a couple of pubs in central Manchester. Within a few weeks, they'd renamed it Whozits, thereby giving it a name all true northerners would never forget. I believe they also toyed with Whatsits, another name people would have no trouble in remembering. If memory serves, I think they kept the place for about five years until the bulldozers moved in. Nowadays, the area around The Picador has changed dramatically and no trace of the club remains. In fact, I think its exact location is now just a piece of empty land near the tram lines running across Shudehill.

The money I got from the sale of The Picador I put towards the purchase of Napoleon's, a pub/restaurant on Sackville Street next-door to Chorlton Street Bus Station, now, of course, right in the middle of Manchester's Gay Village. Back then, even though the area was still popular with the gay community, it could hardly be called a village. Apart from Napoleon's, other nearby pubs such as the Union and the Rembrandt also attracted gays, and these three pubs were really the beginnings of what we know today.

Along with Colin Rigby (who had much more experience of this kind of thing than I did – he already had an interest in a couple of clubs up in Doncaster), I bought Napoleon's from Malcolm Allison, the Manchester City manager, and his business partner Freddie Pye, a City director. Colin had been at an auction one day where he'd met a guy called Billy Kerfoot, who already owned half-a-dozen clubs in Manchester city centre. Amongst others, Billy was acting as an agent for Malcolm and Freddie and one of the places he was currently trying to offload was Napoleon's.

I was driving through town one day with Colin when he suddenly said, 'There's that place Billy Kerfoot's been trying to sell me. Shall we go and have a look?' As Freddie had met Colin previously in the engineering and scrap metal business, he let us have the keys so we went and had a look.

Colin was (and still is) a really good friend whom I'd first met socially at The Rockingham Club back in the mid-1960s. For those who know Colin today, it's hard to believe that for nearly 12 years he was a policeman. Like me, Colin also came from an equally poor, two-up, two-down background and has been known to say that his family was posher than mine. What he really means is that they had flagged floors before they became popular! Although we are as different as chalk and cheese, we just seemed to hit it off immediately and have shared a lot of good times since. We've had some bad times as well, but we can both say that during the 30-odd years we've known each other, we've never had a cross word. We've always stuck together, which I think is marvellous. I think that tells you something about our friendship.

During our friendship, we've also had some wonderful holidays together. Two memorable trips to Madeira spring immediately to mind. Although neither of us at the time were what you might call 'free agents', just the two of us went one year with the idea of trying to get as much sand, sea and sex as we possibly could in a fortnight. We really did have a ball or two. There was one particular lad but, in the end, it turned out he actually fancied a pair of my shoes more than me. I had a lovely bright red pair, the kind that Flamenco dancers wear, as well as a leopard-skin pair with Cuban heels. Nothing bothered me because I was just way over the top camp, and would wear practically anything. This lad and his friends were convinced I was a popstar because of the way I dressed and behaved. Of course, I didn't correct him entirely; what I did say was that I was singer who had his own band. When this story got around, everyone just wanted to hang around and be seen with me. He went on so much about my shoes that, as the holiday was nearing its end, I just gave him a pair and thought that was the end of that. Boy, was I wrong!

Because we'd had such a good time on the island, we decided to go back again the following year. This time, though, I took my partner Alan, and Colin took his partner, Tony. I never even gave the shoes a second thought until, one day, the four of us were walking down the main street in Funchal when, in the distance, I saw these leopard-skin shoes (with Cuban heels) coming towards me with the same boy still wearing them. He was riding his motorbike and had his mother hanging on as a passenger at the back. As the boy started to wave to me, Alan spotted the shoes and recognised them immediately.

'Those are Frank's shoes. What the hell are you doing wearing them?' he yelled at the boy. He went absolutely mad, knocked the boy to the floor, ripped the shoes off his feet and then battered him with them.

Colin has the cheek to say I was fat in those days, but does tell the truth when he says I did go to see a notorious Manchester doctor for some of his fat-reducing pills. I've no idea what was in them (probably amphetamines) and there were bloody hundreds of them, but I did lose quite a bit of weight with them. At one point, I peaked at 18 stones (so I suppose Colin is right) and was far too heavy, so to try and disguise the fact I used to wear a long black coat with a huge stand-up collar. Colin said I looked like the Emperor Ming from *Flash Gordon*. I liked the coat but it is fair to say that they were only mildly popular and even then only in the more outrageous shops. There are some photographs of me when I was, how shall we say, 'larger', but they will never see the light of day as long as I'm still around. If anyone reading this has any, please burn them!

I was told that other people who were seeing the doctor at the same time as me actually lost their lives as well as some weight; one of them on a couch during a party I was at in a house in Hollinwood. The poor sod was lying there for ages before anyone found out he'd gone!

Whilst on the subject of Mr Colin Rigby, let me give you another example of his cheek. Just before Christmas last year, he told me (with a smirk) that he'd worked out my old-age pension for me. He was delighted to tell me my allowance was going to be £98.27 per week. For all his cheek, though, it did bring home to me how quickly time has flown.

Back at Napoleon's, when I first saw it, it looked more like a corner shop than a pub. But then I thought, Well, it's not really me but it's another outlet so we went for it. The idea was that Colin would run Napoleon's and run it purely as a gay club; I'd do an odd spot now and again, but would only retain a financial interest in the place.

Occasionally, I'd do a magic act with the well-known and well-loved Manchester comedian Jackie Carlton. Some people described this as bizarre, while some were a bit more forthright. They said it was bloody hopeless! Jackie spent most of his time accusing me of stealing his act. Naturally, I disagreed with him, saying that our styles were familiar only inasmuch as we both take the piss out of the audience instead of telling them jokes.

We employed a young, straight (well, most of the time!) disc jockey, who went on to work on local radio, by the name of Pete Smith. Pete is still in the business today (and is still playing the same records!), working as he does at The Ritz on Whitworth Street. I think one of the records he still plays today is my version of 'The Old Camp Fire', which, although released back in 1989, has sold literally thousands of copies since. I do know for a fact that it is still played quite a bit in the discos of the Spanish Costas and the Mediterranean islands, because I had a phone call from one of the television holiday programmes not too long ago asking me where they could get hold of a copy. Interestingly enough, even though I think the song is just a bit of harmless fun, it caused quite a stir when it first came out.

The record was produced in a photo sleeve, and featured me (dressed in a strawberry-blonde wig and sequinned evening dress) with half-a-dozen little girls in their Brownie uniforms. Well, various people, including the Brownies Association, described the cover as 'distasteful', and even court action was mentioned because I'd apparently not cleared the use of the uniforms with the correct authorities. One ten-year-old girl featured on the cover actually resigned from the Brownies with her mother's full backing over this ridiculous situation. Even the mother said she thought the whole uproar was very narrow-minded. I just could not believe all this fuss and was amazed as to how the whole innocent thing could be classed as offensive. In the end, I just arranged for new sleeves to be printed. I can easily live without such petty things.

I described Pete back then as 'a very nice little boy. He looks like a jockey waiting for a jump.' We paid him £35 for seven nights' work. Even though the money was poor, Pete is still a good friend today; indeed, he collaborated a great deal with this book, painstakingly trying to make some semblance of order out of my lengthy ramblings, as well as reminding me of events I'd long since forgotten.

The first thing Pete did when we employed him was to complain about the sound system. We had a 40-watt amplifier (which, to be honest, had seen better days) and two 12in speakers. What more could any DJ ask for? Pete also complained about where we asked him to work. We put him right in front of a window that was older than the amplifier and let in even the slightest of breezes. Every night without fail, he'd start on about a 'gale' blowing through, until one night I said to him, 'Oh, stop moaning. I'll go and get you a shawl off my mother.' He never took me up on the offer and, in the end, just got used to it, although to this day he still blames me for his bad back.

One day, Pete came to see Colin and me and told us he'd seen some new equipment. Apparently it was just what was needed and was perfect for the club and for Pete. Now we both knew what he was like when it came to broadcasting and recording gear. Colin said to him, 'You'll have this place looking like bleedin' Home Moss if I let you.'

Pete replied, 'But it's only £150.'

'Only 150 fucking pounds!' I replied almost hysterically.

Pete, trying to make things better, only made it worse by saying, 'And if it breaks down, we've still got the old stuff on standby.'

Well, that was it for Colin. He let rip with, 'For £150, if it fucking breaks down, *you'd* better be on standby!'

In the end, he finally persuaded us to get the gear and it was an immediate improvement and success.

If Pete became well known for playing the records at Napoleon's, then anyone who bought a drink there will certainly remember Alice from behind the bar, Ernie the outrageously camp black chef and another name from the past, Phil Clegg, the doorman. Phil preferred the title of 'Floorwalker'. To him, it sounded much grander. All great characters during what were great times in a great little pub.

While Colin and Pete began to do some really good business and Napoleon's became the number-one gay club in town, I had to put all my efforts into Foo Foo's. Even though I had the final say on things, I left the everyday running of the place to my partner Alan Owen. Alan eventually became my manager as well as the club's, and would arrange all my shows and bookings away from Foo Foo's.

I didn't want it to be specifically a gay club and began almost to select, if you like, the people I'd allow in. I was determined it would be the making of me. When I left Butterworth's back in 1971, the directors kindly agreed to keep my job open should things not work out for me. I couldn't see them still keeping their promise four years later, so I simply had to make Foo Foo's Palace a success. Apart from a bit of money tied up in Napoleon's, I had nothing else to fall back on.

Nowadays, of course, Foo Foo holds court in her palace. Undoubtedly, she is the star, the 'queen', and yet, in 1975, she was also the manager, the cleaner, the pot washer, the barmaid and general dogsbody. Like The Picador, I had no money to take on any staff and once more had to rely on my brothers to help out. Again, like The Picador, I also did my fair share of work on the door as the 'chucker outer'.

When we first opened Foo Foo's, I never stopped working. We opened officially six nights a week, except Sunday. You could open on Sundays then as long as people were sitting down eating and not standing at the bar drinking. In other words, a restaurant was OK, but a pub or nightclub wasn't. I thought the licensing laws were stupid – you could have a drink only if you had some food – so I used to open illegally on Sundays and we treated it as more of a social club with friends of mine just coming in for a quiet drink. One particular Sunday, we were raided by the police and the first thing they did was to rush into the kitchens and check the ovens. Well, of course, they were stone cold; they hadn't been on for the best part of a day. Bob Greaves, the anchorman from *Granada*, was in that night (he became a regular visitor and supporter of the club as time went on) along with some other local radio presenters and, fortunately for me, the police only issued a warning and I got off. But I still had no choice and was forced to close the club in future on Sundays. Technically, this gave me a day off, although invariably all it meant was I'd go and sing somewhere else instead.

Almost from the outset, a large number of my audience was female and primarily from Manchester and the North-West. I must stress that this was in no way deliberate, it was just the way it happened and Foo Foo's soon became *the* place for girls to have their hen parties. It has been said many times that a bride-to-be hasn't had a proper hen party unless she's had it at Foo Foo's.

Because of this I began to get a little bit of notoriety in the papers and started to do some charity work that the papers also picked up on. At the time, I didn't realise how involved in charity work I'd become.

One of my very first charity connections saw me with my own netball team and we raised more than £50,000 for various Manchester causes in the mid-1970s.

I made a single for EMI which would have sold lots more copies had it not been for my foolishness, a fact now I'm not ashamed to admit. They wanted me to go on a publicity tour all over the country and because I was still trying to build Foo Foo's Palace up, because I was still trying to raise my name, I said I didn't want to do it and I really missed the boat.

Another early charity spot took place in February 1977 to try and raise some money for the families of seven women who'd died a few weeks earlier in a factory fire on China Lane, literally just a few yards from the club. I'd decided to stage a show and donate the proceeds to the fund that had been set up and, with the help of pop group Sweet Charity, I did a bit of promotional work beforehand. This involved me appearing in front of a crowd of people on Deansgate and promising to do a strip! However, Deansgate in February is not ideally suited to this, so in the end I faced my audience in a low-cut black evening gown. It was the safest thing for everybody!

Also in 1977, I celebrated my fortieth birthday, although, of course, this fact was only known to a very small number of close personal friends and family. I'd gone to the club as usual in my pink (yes, pink!) Rolls-Royce, only to be told that a birthday party had been laid on for me at my bungalow in

Failsworth, so we all set off up Oldham Road. Only this time we all went back together, not, unfortunately, in the same style as I'd arrived in. We went in Pete Oliver's (from the pop group Sweet Charity) roadie van, a bloody awful thing full of various boxes, bits of guitars, microphones and who knows what else. When we got to the bungalow, Pete and Michael Ryan opened the back doors and I leapt out screaming loudly, 'It's not my van. They've kidnapped me!' just in case any neighbours spotted me getting out of this old heap.

A lot of business at the club came almost from the first week it opened literally by word of mouth. Even today, after nearly thirty years, it's still the same. People come to the club, have a good time and then tell someone else. I don't have to do any advertising; the public sells Foo Foo's for me.

My audience has never been exclusively gay. Yes, obviously, they do come to see me when I'm doing a one-man/woman show in a theatre or on stage at Foo Foo's, but I've never played the gay scene exclusively to make my living. The main reason for that is pure and simple – I'm not a mime act. The gay scene has never been short of Shirley Basseys and Tina Turners and, even before that, Dorothy Squires and Dusty Springfields. I'm not an impressionist; I'm an entertainer. If anyone ever asks me, even today, what my show is like, I always give them the same answer: 'You'll have to come and see it. My show is me.' When I perform, I perform. All right, admittedly, there may be a bit of repetition, but 90 per cent of the time, the show is different. That's because the audience, the people and the situation are different.

I realised right at the start of my career that the people who sit in the seats and watch you are the stars of the show. Without them, I'm nothing. If you respect an audience, no matter how big or small, no matter how sophisticated or rough (believe me, my audiences have been right across the board), then they will respect you and, hopefully, come back and see you again. Even today at my age (which, of course, I don't look – I've still got a pretty face) I get proposals from women (and the odd – and the very odd – man) of marriage. This has happened almost from the opening of Foo Foo's. Women are completely mesmerised by the contrast at the end of the show between Foo and Frank. No question, I play up to the women and that's probably the reason why my audiences are mainly female. They can relate to all the beauty, the glamour and the fact that I've got good legs!

One woman in particular liked me so much that she'd come to the club four nights a week along with a friend of hers. Every night without fail, she'd ask me for a signed photograph. This went on for months and months until, one day, I got a phonecall from what turned out to be her husband. This woman had never mentioned she was married and right from the start of the phonecall, I knew what was coming. He said, 'I know you're having an affair with my wife.'

Obviously this came as a shock to me, so I replied, 'I don't know what you're talking about. I don't even know who your wife is.'

We arranged to meet a few days later and he turned up with a photograph of me with his wife taken at the club. When I saw the photo, I recognised the woman immediately and, with nothing at all to hide, told him so. I also told him she was the woman who asks for a signed photo every time she comes in.

He said, 'I know. They're all over our bedroom wall! The only thing she thinks of 24 hours a day is you.' He continued, 'She's now in a psychiatric ward at Crumpsall Hospital because of it. I work nights in a garage and have only just found out about her obsession. I still love my wife but when I found out about this affair, I just couldn't take it.'

I tried to tell him that there was nothing going on and this 'affair' was all in his wife's mind. I'd certainly not done anything to egg her on. He went on to say he didn't want to leave his wife and I reassured him that he didn't have to. I said, 'Look, when are you going to the hospital next?' He said he was going later that afternoon and I told him I'd meet him there. I said, 'You just get yourself there and leave the rest to me.'

When I got to the hospital, my first stop was to speak to the ward sister and let her know what I planned to do. Once this had been sorted out, I went into the ward where the husband was already sitting on the edge of his wife's bed. From looking very depressed, the woman's face lit up when she saw me coming in. I asked her how she was and she replied she was fine and then I said, 'You've been telling your husband lies. You're telling him that you're having an affair with me. But I've got a shock for you now. I *am* having an affair – but I'm having it with your husband!' I went on, 'You should have realised after all these years you've been coming to the club that I just wanted to be friends with you and your girlfriend. I'm friends with lots of ladies, but it doesn't mean I want sexual relationships with them. But the sheer fact that you left your husband and he then contacted me, well, we've been seeing each other.'

At this point she turned to her husband and said, 'Are you gay?'

The husband was totally gobsmacked! He didn't know what to say or do, because I hadn't warned him in advance of what I was going to say. I helped him out. I said to his wife, 'No he's not gay – he's just lonely. All the time you've been coming to the club, you've been neglecting him. You've got this fantasy in your mind of sleeping with me and it's all wrong. The next time you come to my club, you'll come with your husband. You'll come as a couple and, if you don't, then I won't let you in and I'll never, ever, speak to you again.'

She then broke down in tears and her husband put his arms around her and they cried together. After a few minutes, I said, 'I'll now tell you the truth. I haven't been having an affair with your husband – or anyone else for that matter. My job is to entertain people and make them laugh. It's certainly not to split people up.'

The outcome of all this is that the woman got better and, I'm delighted to say, has been back to the club many times since, every time with her husband.

When I'm in full drag on stage at Foo Foo's with a hen party or two in attendance, I'm in my element. I can stand in front of these women, sometimes wearing a dress that can cost more money than they earn in three months, be outrageously rude to them and they love it. I'll get the prospective bride up on stage and say things like, 'She must be Scandinavian. Hasn't she got a lovely face for an 'orse?' Or I'll ask if it's to be a white wedding. When I'm told 'yes', I ask them if they are marrying a poof! The beauty of all this is I'm not doing anything they don't want me to. I get letters in advance from people in the bride's party who tell me certain things; I'll 'earwig' their conversations as I'm walking through the club and I get all my staff to do the same. When I get up on stage, I'm already armed with all this information and I use every bit of it. However, I know exactly how far to go with it and I do it all in good fun. I never go out intentionally to hurt or offend anyone maliciously.

At the end of the show, I always come back on stage dressed as Frank, in a black tuxedo. I love to see the expressions on these ladies' faces, especially by now as they've had more than a few drinks. They always ask me the same three questions: 'Are you married?' 'Have you got an girlfriend?' and 'Are you homosexual?' I always give them the same answer – 'I'm too busy to be married or homosexual.' They can make their own conclusions from that!

People are used to me nowadays, but when I first started out I'd get some very funny looks when I went shopping. Dressed as Frank I used to go to Boots and experiment with the make-up and then across to Kendal's where I'd try on a few gowns. One day, I was trying on a pair of high-heeled shoes in Kendal's when a posh woman customer shouted at me, 'What do you think you're doing?' I looked across at her and said, 'If you could earn as much as I shall in these tonight, then you'd buy a pair as well!' I'm not sure if she really understood what I meant by it, but at least it shut her up.

I have to be very careful when it comes to buying shoes because I occasionally suffer – despite my youth – with gout, an affliction usually associated with the more senior amongst us. I remember one instance a few years ago when I had a really bad attack and had to buy a new pair of shoes every single day purely because I had to cut them up to get them on. Even though I was in considerable pain, I was determined not to let it get the better of me and continued with my commitments. I did a rugby club presentation at the Lightbowne Hotel in Moston at the request of a friend of mine, Jackie Richmond. At the end of the evening, a bunch of these rugby players marched up on stage and lifted me high up above their heads and I thought to myself, Please don't drop me with my feet! I honestly thought if they did, I'd never get up again.

Sometimes I will admit to being a bit of a devil, but I don't class myself as a freak. I'm just an ordinary bloke who makes a living wearing women's frocks! During the punk era, I'd see these kids with spiked hair all covered in chains and think to myself, Now that looks freakish. How could they be seen out dressed like that?

In January 1986, another shopping trip of mine warranted a mention in the national press. I was asked to attend the wedding of some friends of mine, pub landlady Pat Harvey and her boyfriend Ron Knox. Nothing unusual about that, you may think, but I was asked to be a *bridesmaid*! Like anything else I do, I took it very seriously and went out and bought a new sequinned dress for £3,000. I didn't think anything of it, but at least it got my name in the papers again! I was also a bridesmaid (but never the bride!) again the following year when I volunteered my services to former Manchester United boss Tommy Docherty and his wife-to-be Mary Brown. Although he was initially taken by surprise, Tommy laughed and then said, 'Well, it should make for a very interesting day.'

On more than one occasion, men who are not gay, who've not had the experience, stay behind after the show just to talk to me. They tell their taxi or coach or whatever to carry on without them; they're quite happy just to stay and have a chat. Although they see me as Foo all night, and then Frank, I think sometimes they find it hard to tell the difference. These men tell me some of the most intimate things, almost confiding in me, if you like, and I think it's the female side of me, Foo, that brings it out. I could never see them telling straight men some of the things they tell me. Sometimes, I have to say, it does get a bit frightening.

A few months after the woman with the 'obsession', some time during the summer of 1996, I think it was, another person took a fancy to me, although this time it was much more sinister and I had to involve the police. Someone began to follow me daily wherever I went in the car. I drove a white Bentley turbo at the time. When I left the house, the club or simply driving through town, there was this same car – a silver-green metallic Ford Corsair – constantly in the rear-view mirror. What made it even more sinister was the fact that the car had tinted windows, so I had no idea just how many people were in it. He (I assumed it was a 'he') never got close enough for me to stop my car and get out and challenge him. Every time I stopped he'd shoot off down the nearest side street and I'd lose him. Eventually, after weeks and weeks, I finally managed to get the number plate and I phoned the police. I had to because, by now, I was getting very worried, especially late at night during the long drives back from central Manchester to my home in Shuttleworth. I must admit the murder of my good friend and fellow club owner Colin Murphy just a couple of years earlier sprang to mind on more than one occasion. The full story of this tragic incident I'll come to later.

A few days went by before the police eventually pulled him. They came to the club to tell me the news and said, 'We've caught him, Frank, and there's nothing to be worried about. He's a married man and because of his wife, he doesn't want to approach you. He means you no harm – he's just besotted with ladies underwear and with you!' I thought it was a very weird situation; but can you really blame him for being besotted with one so lovely? I think he just wanted to try my knickers on, but didn't have the courage to come right out and ask me.

The vast majority of my audience at the club is – and always has been – aged between 18 and 25. This is simply because we have built up such a good reputation for being able to provide a great night out with Foo Foo's being constantly packed out with weddings, birthday parties and hen nights. I've no doubt in my mind at all that the fact we attract such a young audience has kept me young as well. I'll never grow old with the sort of audiences I attract. That's where I differ – and I mean no disrespect here; I love him to bits – from Danny La Rue. If you go and see one of Danny's shows today, the audience will be full of what is commonly known as the 'blue-rinse' brigade, primarily ladies of 60–65 and upwards. But they are still lovely people and Danny can still pack them in, so the whole thing is obviously still popular; it's just a completely different package to the one I offer.

Having said that, though, I did try to do a show once with

Danny; the idea was that we'd join forces to raise money for the soldiers serving in the Gulf. We had to postpone the show initially, as Danny had to fly to Australia for a cabaret tour, so we made plans to get together when he returned. In the end, though, for various reasons, nothing ever happened, which I still think is a shame because I know it would have been a great show.

It was due largely to one particular hen party that Foo Foo's Palace really took off. It was a really good night, a Saturday, and the club was packed out. The following Monday, I had fantastic coverage – both on the front and in the centre pages – of the *Guardian* newspaper, no less. It turned out that the mother of one of the girls in the hen party was, if memory serves, an editor at the paper. She, too, had been in the audience and wrote all this glowing stuff about me, the club and what a great time everyone had had. I couldn't have written anything better myself and, of course, it was marvellous publicity for the club. She used phrases like, 'What has this man got?' 'Why do women follow this man?' and 'Who is Foo Foo?'

Within a few days of the article, I had people from the flagship of the BBC's nightly news and current affairs programme *Nationwide* phoning me up and asking if they could make a documentary about me. Well, naturally, I was a bit shy at first, but eventually agreed! The documentary took me back to Butterworth's, to the cotton mill, to Mill Street and to all my old haunts. Once the show was broadcast on prime-time television, the audiences began to come from all over the country. Even today, every week without fail, we can have coach parties from as far away as Bristol and Newcastle for hen parties. The *Nationwide* broadcast certainly put Foo Foo's Palace and Frank Lammar firmly on the national map.

Up until this point, any money I made from the club went straight back into the fixtures and fittings. Because of all this free publicity, we began to do a roaring trade – much better that I had ever dreamt of – and so I thought, Sod it, I'll treat myself, and promptly went out and had a load of new frocks professionally made by local dressmaker Louise Roberts.

Not long after all this publicity, I was having a drink one night in Napoleon's when Danny La Rue swept in complete with entourage, including dancer Lionel Blair. Danny was then appearing at the Palace Theatre on Oxford Road. People had told him who I was and about the little nightclub I had and, although we'd never met before, we just got chatting and Danny later invited me to go and see his show and to call him 'Dan'. He insists all his friends call him Dan.

So I went, saw the show and loved everything about it. Danny's act and material were nothing like mine, but what I loved more than anything was the glamour and panache of the whole thing. The style, the stage, the whole package convinced me. I said to myself, 'That's what I want.' It was a turning point for me, so I went back determined to improve both me and the club.

I went into debt and spent £150,000 on extending it and it really stretched me for a while. I refurbished The Ranch Bar area of the club, purely for the new punk rock explosion that was coming through at the time. Salford-born Mike Sweeney and his band The Thunderbirds regularly rehearsed in The Ranch Bar in preparation for their many gigs in and around the

North-West. This was of course in the days before he became a hugely popular DJ with Manchester's Piccadilly Radio prior to joining Capital Gold in London.

In July 1976, I recorded my first album (with a narration by newsreader John Mundy from BBC Television in Manchester), *Foo Foo Lammar Live at the Palace.* The album contained several tracks, including favourites such as 'On a Wonderful Day Like Today' and 'This Is My Life'. It didn't do a great deal in the charts (I don't even think it got into them!) but it sold a few copies and I don't remember losing too much money on the deal.

The punk era was relatively short-lived as far as the club was concerned and so, later (as the popularity of Foo Foo's increased), we lost The Ranch Bar completely and made the entire club Foo Foo's, big enough to sit and feed more than 600 people, as well as to put on a full stage show.

From the early days, Foo Foo's also became popular with the showbiz fraternity, as stars appearing at Manchester's Palace Theatre and Opera House would regularly call in for a drink. They would telephone in advance to see if they could come in and, of course, visits from these people only created welcome publicity and increased the club's popularity even more. It was a great feather in my cap to be able to attract some of the top names in the entertainment industry. Victor Spinetti, John Inman, Bonnie Langford and, of course, Danny La Rue all became regulars at the club, as well as very good friends. Larry Grayson, who was a huge star then with *The Generation Game*, and Barbara Windsor of *Carry On* and (later) *EastEnders* fame were also frequent visitors, and the beauty of all this was that they all came on the recommendations of their fellow artistes. These were brilliant times with brilliant people.

For a good few years, I also hosted *Foo Foo's Pantomime Night* at the club and would throw open my doors to the entire cast of all the pantos on their last night in Manchester. As well as the stars mentioned above, other welcome visitors included Bruce Forsyth, Les Dawson and Ken Dodd, and what looked like a remake of the television show *The Comedians*, with Mick Miller, Johnny Casson, Norman Collier and Manchester's own Bernard Manning.

I saw Larry Grayson on and off over the next few years; the last time was at a party at The Dorchester Hotel in London following the Royal Variety show in November 1993. I mentioned to him that I intended to stage a show at Manchester's Palace Theatre the following April in aid of Pendlebury Children's Hospital. Larry said he'd not played the Palace for years and would love to have another go, so we tentatively arranged a comedy sketch that involved him telling a few gags and joining me in a song. Tragically, Larry was to pass away in January, so he never got the chance to fulfil his long-standing ambition. He was a lovely man and I had lost a good friend.

It was around this time that Les Dawson bought me a Capo di Monte figure for my birthday. It was a Napoleonic war soldier and it began a kind of trend, I suppose, because without fail, every year since, friends have bought me more. I've got upwards of 30 of these now.

Jeremy Beadle, star of television's *You've Been Framed!*, was another visitor to the club. Every time Jeremy was in

Manchester, he'd call in to see me and every time he'd say the same thing: 'There's got to be a spot for you on television. We've got to find you something.' At one point, it was hoped that Jeremy would be able to revive the 1960s American TV game show *Queen for a Day*, and he had me in line for the host. The idea of the show was that ordinary women are given a complete makeover and the chance to win some luxurious prizes. I must admit I did fancy the idea but, in all honesty, would any of the contestants really have looked as glamorous as me?

As time went on, I was offered television work (and plenty of it), but it was all down in London and I wasn't prepared to leave Foo Foo's Palace. Purely and simply, because of the Palace, I'd at last become 'somebody' and I remained loyal to it. Without being arrogant, if I wasn't on, then there was no show. Ironically, Frank was no one without the Palace and the Palace was nothing without Frank.

Years later, I was offered a presenting job on *The Big Breakfast* for Channel 4; this was after Paula Yates had left the show. They said to me, 'We want you, as Foo Foo, to lie on the bed and introduce things and generally say whatever comes into your head.' Even though the money was certainly not to be sniffed at, this would have meant me living in London and getting up at 4.00 every morning, what with the make-up and everything, in readiness for the show. 'No, sorry, not for me,' I told them, 'but thanks anyway.' In the end they offered the job to another relative unknown – Paul O'Grady, alias Lily Savage. Paul wasn't new to me, though, because he'd worked for me years before at Foo Foo's and I knew just what he was capable of.

Paul/Lily took the job and so began a great career that would eventually lead to *Blankety Blank* as well as his own shows. And good luck to him. At the time I turned it down, people said I was bloody stupid and that I should have taken the job. Those same people also ask me if I'm envious of Paul. In all honesty, I have to say no I'm not, and I'm not just saying that because we are good friends. It was my decision to turn the job down; Paul had no bearing on it at all. Although he wears posh frocks like I do (not as good quality, mind), he does a different kind of act to me and, as I always say, 'There's enough work for everyone to go round.' If there is one slight gripe I do have, it's that when Paul finally reached the big time the television people made *Lilydrome*; in my opinion, that was just a copy of Foo Foo's Palace. That really was a show made for me; it was the spot Jeremy Beadle had always said was there for me. It wasn't Paul's fault; it wasn't Lily's fault. It was my fault. I wouldn't go to London. It was purely my decision. I was happy in my work and where I was. I had a Rolls-Royce, a big house and my own little empire. It was as simple as that, but sometimes, looking back, I do wonder what would have happened if I'd have taken the chance and left Manchester for the big time.

In 1998, I did have a brief flirtation with television when I filmed *Foo Foo's Party Night* for Granada's *Men and Motors* satellite channel. The show went out on Friday nights for eight weeks and featured both the club and my life outside. The show was advertised as 'honest vulgarity', a phrase that summed everything up perfectly.

Anyway, I'm nowhere near finished yet and I'm determined

to do more work on national television before I'm done. Foo Foo's Palace has been a wonderful place for me and brought me many, many things, things I never even dreamt of when growing up in Ancoats. I suppose the fact that the club has depended on me entirely for its success has, in some way, hindered my career on a national level. Like all good things, though, my association with the little club downstairs on Dale Street must come to an end and that time will be in December 2002. That's when the lease is up – after an amazing 27 years. God alone knows where the time has gone. In 2003, I'm hoping to achieve my goals on television and to take my one-man/woman show on a national tour of theatres. But all that is in the future; let's get back to the past.

Despite turning down offers of work in London, I did manage to do other things in Manchester. In 1984 one such show was *The Rocky Horror Picture Show* produced by The Library Theatre Company. The producers of the show came to the club to see me perform and then offered me the part of the corseted and whip-wielding Frank N Furter. At least no one could say I got the part because I looked too normal! When they gave me the script, I thought, What the bloody hell is all this about? because at that time I'd never heard of *The Rocky Horror Show.* Mind you, as Frank N Furter is described as 'creator of the body-beautiful ideal man', I suppose the part could have been written for me! We did five weeks at the Wythenshawe Forum and then we took the full show to the Palace Theatre for two more. We were sold out for the entire seven-week period.

I thought at first we might go straight to the Palace Theatre with the show (which, by the way, I already had booked for *The Foo Foo Lammar Show* for two nights a few weeks later) but was told by the producers that initially we needed a smaller, more intimate kind of setting. The main reason for this is that my character, Frank N Furter, had to make his entrance through the audience and the size and opulence of the Palace was thought to be too much. When we did take the show there, I suggested we changed his entrance. I said, 'Let's bring him down in a lift.' So I got the fire brigade in. I knew this would work and, even if I say so myself, I made a fantastic entrance. Even though I knew nothing at all about it, I saw *Rocky Horror* as a challenge and that's why I took the part. It was the first time I'd ever worked with a script and the first time I'd ever had a director telling me what to do. Even though I have done other scripted shows since, *Rocky Horror* was the only one I've ever kept to. All the others start wandering off almost from the first night! The show finished at about 10.00pm each night and then I'd rip off the suspenders and corset, throw down the whip (well, most of the time!) and rush back to the club for a quick change into Foo Foo.

About three years after I did *Rocky Horror*, I hoped once again to do some work with The Library Theatre in a production of the famous *La Cage Aux Folles*. The idea was that I'd play the part of an ageing transvestite club owner (perfect casting, some might say) called Albin in a copy of a bejewelled, white chiffon frock worn some 40 years earlier on stage by the actress Jill Summers. This was one of many parts Jill played in theatres before she became better known as Phyllis Pearce in *Coronation Street*. Jill actually presented me with a signed photograph of herself wearing the dress, which, even back then in 1947, cost £400 to be made. I calculated it would have cost me around £5,000 to have reproduced it, but in the end the production never took off, which I felt was a great pity as the ladies in the audience would have loved that frock.

All my life, I've looked forward to new and different challenges. This book, too, was also a challenge. Over the last few years, many people (especially my great friend, the lovely Susie Mathis) have suggested to me that I should write my life story and, finally, I thought if I don't do it now, my mind will be too far gone to remember much about it!

I've known Susie for probably more years than either of us care to remember. We did a show together once at the Palace Theatre about six months before I did *Rocky Horror*. Susie was having some terrible problems with her marriage at the time and I decided she needed cheering up so I booked the theatre and we did this show for charity. There was only one small snag; I'd no idea at all what was going to be in the show. It just never entered my head until I'd actually made the booking. That's just the way I am sometimes. I'm not that well known for my forward planning! Fortunately, Susie and Michael Ryan, my manager, rallied round and we managed eventually to come up with a show that was not only very good, but also very successful and raised a lot of money for charity.

It was called *Foo and Sue* and we had a lot of fun doing it, one memorable sketch being a mickey-take (without the ice) of the ice-skating champions Jane Torville and Christopher Dean called *Orville and Queen*. We rehearsed for ages prior to the show with Susie insisting we copied Torville and Dean exactly, right down to the smallest twist, turn and lift. I remember we combined some of the rehearsals with a trip to Gran Canaria, the idea being that we could practise the lifts and the soft sand would act as a cushion in case of any drops. I think we had about half-an-hour's serious practice before I'd had enough; I wanted to get on with the holiday and have a good time!

Susie stayed in a hotel while I stayed in the apartment block next-door. In between the two buildings were some palm trees and, after a few drinks (too many actually!), we decided it would be great fun to try and climb to the top of one of them. It wasn't bloody funny when we got stuck at the top, though! Susie insists I spent my time in captivity flashing at passing holidaymakers. I, for my part, remember getting stuck, but nothing else. I ask you, the reader – going on my past record – to make your own mind up on this!

If I don't remember that event, I certainly do remember another one on that same trip. We were out one afternoon just having a nice stroll in the sunshine along the seafront, when I had the worst kind of accident imaginable. Susie was chatting to Billy and Colin Rigby and some other friends of ours and I'd walked on a few paces in front when I let out a tremendous fart. Or at least I thought I had. Susie noticed the smell immediately and the stain on the back of my beige-coloured trousers was also a bit of a giveaway. It was a terrible situation and the only way out of it (at least as far as I could see at the time) involved Susie. I managed to persuade her to sit down on the little seafront wall and I climbed up behind her and sat on her shoulders. When I think back now to what she must have felt like, it must have been awful for her. At the time, though, I had other, more pressing things on my mind. She then tottered across the street with me to a little clothes shop where I snatched a pair of trousers off the peg and rushed into the changing rooms. As quickly and as carefully as I could, I took the soiled ones off and put the new ones on. I then paid the man at the till and left the shop. Of course, I didn't tell him I'd left the other pair in the changing cubicle! Can you imagine the shock on the next customer's face? You might find this hard to believe, but I've never been back to that shop since.

The day before we were due to return home was Billy's birthday. I arranged for a cake and we all had photographs taken in our white suits and pastel colours as the sun was setting. It was a lovely way to end a lovely trip. We then played charades for a while before the evening meal. Even though the eating did eventually finish, the drinking didn't. As time went on, we all got more and more silly and began to throw things at each other. First it was bits of cheese, then it was the éclairs, then it was the chocolate cake and, finally, the birthday cake was used to redecorate the room. Everybody tried to be more outrageous than everyone else but, in the end, and I've said this many times before, 'Nobody out does Foo Foo.' I even smeared a huge piece of cake right across Susie's face, although I did also offer to lick it off!

The apartment was in a terrible state but, and this is the honest truth, we did clean up every little bit before we left for the airport. What we didn't even try to clean up, though, before we left, were our clothes. These had started out as pastel colours to show off our glorious suntans and ended up chocolate, strawberry and lime flavour. They were so far beyond salvation all we could do was to throw them in the bin.

Back home, Susie had previously had Robin Cousins as a guest on her radio show and somehow she managed to persuade him to record our introduction for the opening night. Despite Susie wanting to do everything properly and ever so straight, I wanted to bring a bit of comedy into the proceedings. By the time I'd dropped her once or twice and lost my wig, I think she understood what was going on. At the end, we got a standing ovation, so I think the audience liked it. Susie was a real taskmaster and put a lot of hard work and effort into all the choreography she staged, not least the *Riverdance* sketch. Unfortunately for her, I treated it exactly the same as I'd done the ice-skating routine and my performance bore no resemblance to what we'd actually rehearsed.

Susie, a former Paper Doll and Piccadilly Radio presenter, also worked with me for a while in a kind of double-act show we did at City Lights in Farnworth. I think it was towards the end of 1985 and we became so close that some people suggested there was something more to our relationship than just a friendship.

We both denied these rumours and, anyway, I know that I was far too rude for her (although I did make her laugh a lot) and she was only interested in my jewellery – the gold kind!

Another occasion we worked together (this must have been 1987 or thereabouts) was for the children's charity ChildLine when we did a show at Foo Foo's to try and raise money to go towards their services in Blackley and Eccles.

Susie and her boyfriend Tony Ingham (then head of Piccadilly Radio) stayed with me for a while just after Christmas once, while waiting to move into their new house near Warrington. Although they were living under the same roof as me, because of the different hours we both worked, we hardly ever saw one another. I was quoted in the *Manchester Evening News* as saying, 'We haven't got round to making puff pastry together or whipping each other with scented lettuce leaves.' Don't think we ever did, either! Still, who knows what the future holds? Maybe the next time we share the same roof we'll be in an old folks' home and can get up to a whole manner of mischief.

Even though there has never been any hint of romance between us (apart from an occasional lust on my part), we most certainly are very, very good friends and have worked together for various charities regularly in the years since. I was proud to act as witness for Susie and Tony when they finally did get married, although I did hope I'd get the job of bridesmaid! In the end, I had to settle for driving her to the service in my Rolls and will also admit to crying when I saw her in her wedding dress. I'll also admit to trying to talk her out of it right up until the very last minute but it was no good; in the end, she still went through with it. I'm sure she thought at the time I was joking, but I was deadly serious.

In the following years, Susie suffered terribly as Tony embarked on a string of affairs. The final straw came after about eight years of marriage when he took up with a 24-year-old barmaid from Susie's local. Susie was devastated. All those years had finally caught up with her. Within minutes of her telephoning me, I was round at her place, packed an overnight bag for her and put her up in a hotel. I was as angry as she was devastated.

The next morning, I went back to Susie's house armed with a mutual friend and a supply of black bin bags. Between us, we emptied every single piece of Tony's clothes from the wardrobes into the bin bags before loading them into the car. I then drove to his office and, in front of his work colleagues, I took great pleasure in hurling all the bin bags through his office door.

On a cheerier note, for the Christmas pantomime season in 1996, I did get the chance to chase after Susie in my underwear. We did an adult version of *Peter Pan* for six weeks at Park Hall in Warrington with me playing both the dastardly villain Captain Sling Your Hook and Tonkerbell and Susie playing the always fully-clothed title role. Apart from giving me the chance to cavort round the stage semi-naked, it was also a rare opportunity for me to tackle a butch role. This required little acting on my part. Mind you, I still got to wear a lovely curly wig!

When we first announced our intentions to stage the show, certain members of Warrington Council thought that our version of the children's classic story would be far too risqué. However, thanks to the efforts of lots of people and Liz Dawn in particular, we managed to persuade them that it would be a very funny show and would not offend anyone. Just to confirm how certain we were about it, we even arranged for the Lady Mayoress of Warrington, Mary Roblin, to have front row seats for the opening night. After the show, she told us how much she'd enjoyed it, so despite the initial misgivings, everything turned out fine in the end. As the nights went on, I drifted further and further away from the original script and I suppose got naughtier at the same time. I would have been very disappointed had the show not gone ahead, especially as it was all in aid of the Broken Wings appeal.

It was just a few weeks after Susie and Tony had got married and moved out that I had an encounter with the Metropolitan Police at Euston Station. I'd gone down to London as Michael Crawford had invited Susie to the opening night of *The Phantom of the Opera*. It was about midnight when I realised I should by then have been on the train heading back to Manchester. I managed to get across London and literally leapt on the train just as it was pulling out. About three hours into the journey, I had a feeling that something wasn't quite right and asked the guard how long it would be before we got to Manchester. He said, 'A long time – we're going to Inverness!' So I had to get off and make my way back to London.

Unfortunately, the next Manchester-bound train wasn't for the best part of two hours, so I just dossed down in the station and waited. It was then that the police moved me on; they thought I was some kind of vagrant! Bloody cheek! And this was after I'd spent an extra 50 quid on another ticket home. When I got back and began to tell the story, people asked me why I hadn't taken the Rolls. The answer was simple; just three days before, a lorry had backed into it and caused £6,000 worth of damage. I can still see it now with its legs in the air and its eyelashes on the floor. It wasn't the best of weeks for me.

I think the next time I saw Michael would have been at a Variety Club of Great Britain tribute luncheon held in his honour at the Piccadilly Hotel. It was a huge function broadcast by Granada Television and was presented by Susie. I knew she had to be on her best behaviour because the cameras were there and she was interviewing Michael just before we all sat down to eat. Now Susie and I go back a long way. We have a wonderful relationship but I cannot resist playing practical jokes on her. The fact that this was a serious moment for her made no difference to me; I saw my opportunity and took it. As she was chatting in front of the camera to Michael, I spotted she'd noticed me out of the corner of her eye. Quick as a flash (so to speak), I opened my fly and pissed all over the plant decorations just at her side but off camera. Being the trouper she is, she managed to finish the interview before she came looking to throttle me. She wasn't too pleased with me but I just couldn't resist it!

At the time of doing the regular Wednesday show with Susie, I was actually part-owner of City Lights with a man called Colin Murphy. Colin – all 25st of him – was a real Cockney who was involved in a few clubs and we decided we'd buy the old Blighty's Club and rename it. We spent more than £1 million between us on refurbishment, with a quarter of that amount going on new lighting alone. The club had been converted from an old church and was said to be standing in the middle of a graveyard. During the refurbishment one huge workman was so frightened he was physically sick when he said he saw the ghost of a long-departed woman. Fortunately, I never saw anything at all along these lines and tried to play it all down by jesting, 'Well, if she does appear again, we'll just do the show as *The Sisters Grimm!*'

We managed to persuade the legendary Gloria Gaynor to appear at City Lights in the summer of 1986. The newspapers ran a story saying that she was going to slap my wrists for my recording a version of her classic song 'I Am What I Am' on an album I'd released earlier, which sold 15,000 copies. Of course, she never said any such thing and was really great when she was there. I was also quoted as saying, 'She's had so many hits that Gloria Gaynor, it makes me want to smack her in the gob!' Maybe that was the reason she didn't say anything! 'I Am What I Am' has since become my theme tune and I often think it would make a great title for a book!

Colin Murphy and I once again joined forces when we bought the rundown Tiffany's nightclub in Rochdale. If memory serves, I think it must have been some time in early 1987 because I can remember opening it that same June after we'd had some problem over the liquor licence. We spent £120,000 actually buying the place and then a further £500,000 on doing it up and renamed it Fatso's after Colin and not, as many people suggested, after the local MP Cyril Smith. I invited about 600 people to the opening do, including a lot of celebrities from the showbiz world, and many of these had to travel long distances to get there. It was terrible for me when I got there in the afternoon – along with a new £1,500 frock, bought especially for the occasion – only to find all the doors locked and bolted. The authorities refused to let anyone in because of the confusion with the licence and we had to call the whole thing off just hours before the club was due to open. I was absolutely livid at the time but, fortunately, we managed to get things sorted out and opened the following week with no more problems.

And what a night we had! Those extra few days were well worth the wait. My good friends from *Coronation Street* turned out in force, including Liz Dawn, Michael Le Vell (Kevin Webster), Helen Worth (Gail Tilsley, as she was then) and her energetic screen husband Brian, actor Chris Quentin. Susie Mathis was also on hand and perhaps the highlight of the evening for many was seeing her literally thrown around the dance floor by Chris who completed the performance by doing a cartwheel. Kevin Kennedy (aka Curly Watts) was there as well but put his lack of dancing down to many late nights looking after his recently-born son Ryan.

I think I'm right in saying that Fatso's was Colin's last involvement with the club scene. In the early hours of a Sunday morning in July 1994, he was attacked and murdered as he arrived home at his house in Eastwood, near Todmorden. It seems that he'd just won around £3,000 at the Sergeant York Casino in Cheetham Hill and had been followed home by some thugs. They waited until he'd got out of his car before hitting him in the face with a shotgun and then made off with his winnings. Colin died the next day in hospital from internal bleeding. To me, it was an absolutely pointless death. Despite his size, Colin really was the proverbial gentle giant and would simply have handed over the money if they'd have told him to.

I knew that violence in clubs had become much worse than when I had first started out and, consequently, I never carried a great deal of money around with me. Colin, on the other hand, was completely the opposite and lots of people knew this. In the end, I suppose, it was his undoing. He was only 53 and we'd been good friends for over 25 years. I was so incensed with the killing that I put up some reward money of £10,000 to find the killers. Unfortunately, not even this made any difference;

the killers are still at large today and I don't think the police are any nearer to finding them.

I personally have two opinions on this terrible tragedy; unfortunately, neither of them can be backed up with a shred of evidence. I think it was either a lover's tiff or an intended robbery that went horribly wrong.

Whilst I'm on the subject of the police, I'm reminded also of the time I became involved with John Stalker, Kevin Taylor and The Quality Street Gang. I'd been invited to a birthday party at Kevin Taylor's house and, to be honest, I didn't know the majority of people there. It was at the time when they were trying to pin something on John Stalker and everything blew up at this party. I later did a show at the Palace Theatre with Susie Mathis to try and raise money for Stalker's legal fees and I think we raised somewhere in the region of £20,000.

My connections with other clubs meant that I was now being seen at other places apart from my spiritual home. One show I did away from Foo Foo's was *A Tribute to Bette Midler*. It was produced by Granada to promote a film she had just released at the time. I can't think why they offered it to me (or even remember the film come to that) but it was a good little show and I enjoyed doing it.

In 1996 I also starred alongside Edward Woodward in a couple of episodes of his BBC television show *Common As Muck* when he played a binman. In one particular episode, he went into a gay club and came across (so to speak) me, in my role as an over-the-top nightclub owner. As if! Not surprisingly, Edward's character Nev took a fancy to me immediately. We shot some scenes in Manchester city centre and some others not too far from where I was living at the time, Shuttleworth, up on the tops near Ramsbottom. Before anyone says anything, I bought the farmhouse because I liked it and not because of the name of the nearby town!

On another occasion, the people of the North-West saw me on television in a *Children in Need* appeal one year. Susie Mathis was hosting the show from Manchester and I was on right at the start, around 7.00pm. I then went to do a show, getting back into Manchester well after midnight and Susie was still on. So I drove back to Oxford Road and finished the show with her in the small hours. You know me; anything for Susie and anything for charity.

Not too long after *Common As Muck*, there was some controversy about billboard advertisements for Black Death vodka. They used me on some of the posters dressed in a feather boa, lingerie and suspenders, obviously a very tasteful and inoffensive poster! For the launch in Manchester, they held a party in Cruz 101 and then brought me through the streets in a hearse behind a full procession (including a brass band) to Foo Foo's Palace, causing many people to think I was dead! The advertising slogan said something like 'this drink will change your life'. Some people thought it had changed me for good! It was all good publicity for both the drink and me and my fee for the stunt was in the form of a cheque made out to Pendlebury Children's Hospital. Meanwhile, the other billboards, which featured a semi-nude woman and a completely nude man (except for a strategically placed hat), caused such offence that Manchester City Council was forced to take them down because they received so many complaints.

But going back to those days in the mid-1970s, as I've said, it was very hard and I worked and worked and worked for two reasons. First, I liked it, whether I was being paid anything or not; and second, I wanted to be somebody. It was during this time that I began to get involved in charity work, something I am proud to say that I am still involved with a quarter-of-a-century later. I used to do a lot of fund-raising for a lady called Leisha Wholley who ran the Richmond Hill old folks' home in Broughton, Salford. These were lovely people and came in very handy once when the police threatened to take my driving licence off me for constantly speeding. I had a second-hand Rolls-Royce then; I'd moved on a bit from my Ellis's meat pie van days! Leisha brought a few of the old folks along to the court in Salford to speak on my behalf, which I thought was a lovely gesture. And I got off! By way of a repayment, I acted as chauffeur when a couple of the 'inmates' got married a few weeks later. They were always popping in and out of each other's rooms although I don't think it was a shotgun job! The gentleman, Bill, was 89 and the lady, Frances, was 91, and I drove them in the Rolls to the Catholic cathedral in Salford for the wedding ceremony. I also bought Frances' wedding outfit for her.

One of the better-known charities I do a lot of work for is The National Association of Guide Dogs for the Blind. I'm always pushing piles of pennies over on their behalf and can assure you there's more than one Labrador out there named Foo Foo after me. It's just my little way of putting something back into a community that has largely, over the years, been very good to me. I like to think I respect people and, in return, I expect respect from others.

I've met some lovely people over the years through my charity work. I did an industry prize-giving lunch once at Manchester's Piccadilly Hotel and the Duke of Westminster was the guest of honour. He just could not get over me; and I did the lunch as Frank, not Foo! Mind you, I did go over the top with him, even though he was royalty. As he was leaving, he said to me, 'Frank, that was marvellous. You must come down to my place in the summer. We're having a charity party in the gardens and I'd love you to meet all my friends.' When the day came round, I was unfortunately ill and had to decline his invitation. As yet, I haven't taken him up on his offer, but I will do.

Certainly not a member of any Royal Family, but nevertheless a tireless charity worker and good friend, is Bernard Manning. Like me, Bernard has come from nothing to being very wealthy but, for all the criticism he takes, he never forgets his roots. We've done a lot of shows together over the years and I can remember back in the mid-1980s we both did a show at our respective clubs to try and raise money for a Wythenshawe man who'd been buried in a pauper's grave in Southern Cemetery. Even in 2000, we promoted overcoats for dogs in our respective football team's colours; Bernard in his blue for City and me in red for United.

Another member of the Royal Family I've had the privilege and pleasure to meet through my charity work is the Duke of Edinburgh. Again, it was at a function at the Piccadilly Hotel where I'd been invited along as a guest. This time, I was told I could take a guest of my own and so I took my mum. Before the meal, the Lord Mayor of Manchester, Alderman Lever, introduced us all to His Royal Highness. Mr Lever said, 'This is Frank Lammar, a very respected celebrity in the north.'

Shaking me by the hand, the Duke said to me, 'And you don't have to tell me who the lady standing next to you is. She is the image of you. It's your dear mother isn't it?' I told him it was and he then went on to Mum. 'And are you enjoying the afternoon?'

'Yes,' she said, 'but the bitter's rotten.'

Slightly taken aback, he said, 'The bitter. Do you mean the beer?'

She replied, 'Yes.'

'Can't you have something else?' the Duke asked.

'Oh no,' she said, 'I don't drink anything else of a lunchtime, only bitter.'

Even though I'd got a bit of a name by then (as well as a Rolls-Royce) and she was talking to royalty, you couldn't change her. My mum was my mum; any wealth, property, even the Rolls-Royce I had, made no difference to Mum.

I bought Mum a little bungalow in Moston and every year I'd take her and her friend Dolores 'Dulla' Rossi from next-door away for a break at Easter. At the time, no licences were allowed for Good Friday and Maundy Thursday, so I used to close the club completely for a few days. We would go to Tenerife (primarily because we could guarantee good weather and also the place is flat) and no matter what money I gave her to spend on herself, she never did. Every penny or peseta would be spent on the grandchildren and we'd come back loaded with presents.

In July 1987, Mum, who was by now 70, fancied a few days in the sun but, owing to work commitments, this time I couldn't go with her. She wasn't feeling too good, anyway, and we all thought a holiday to Tenerife would be just the tonic she needed. How wrong could we be! She'd been there just four days when she slipped on a banana skin and broke a knee. The injury meant she had to be taken to a hospital high up in the mountains for an operation.

I got a phonecall at home telling me what had happened, then I rang my brothers and we were all at Manchester Airport within a matter of hours ready for the next flight out. I'd arranged for an ambulance to be waiting for us at the airport when we got back and then took Mum to a specialist just to check that the operation had been a success. Fortunately, everything turned out OK and we eventually got her back to the comfort and safety of her bungalow in Moston.

As for me, I put in an insurance claim for £1,500 for all the travelling and inconvenience caused and began to try and rearrange the shows I'd cancelled. I was worried my audiences thought I'd just gone off to the beach, but when the story got out in the press, everyone was really supportive and lots of people kept asking me how Mum was. It was ironic that, by rearranging these shows, I had to miss the holiday I'd planned that year – to Tenerife, of all places!

I saw Mum nearly every day, even when I was working. More often than not, I'd go round to her house for lunch and tea every day; in between times, I'd drop her off in the Rolls at either Newton Heath or Grey Mare Lane market, so she could do her shopping. Afterwards I'd give her a lift to her favourite pub, Billy Green's on Rochdale Road in Collyhurst, where she'd meet up with my brothers for a few drinks and I'd drive into Manchester for my work at Foo Foo's.

There was a barmaid who worked at Billy Green's called Diane and I was very jealous of her tits. Every time I saw her, I'd tease her by saying, 'If I was straight, I'd have you.'

For all the literally thousands of times I've given Mum lifts over the years to wherever she wanted to go, I do know that she never liked my driving. She would always say I was an impatient driver. Looking back, I suppose I tried to take Dad's place when he died; I tried to make sure she had everything she needed. I also tried to make up for the rougher times we'd had when we were all growing up. We were always fed and clean, but we never really had anything of value. Now things had changed, I was determined to try and make things better for Mum after all the hard times she'd gone through.

I don't know whether she needed a mink coat or not, but I bought her one for her seventieth birthday. We had a party for her at the club, complete with a wonderful buffet, and I'd invited everyone, from friends and neighbours to the most famous people I knew. I also bought her new shoes and a matching handbag and arranged for her to have her hair done specially. On the way down to town, she said to me, 'I want to stop at Yates's. I want to see Mary Barrow and have a drink with her.' So, complete in mink coat, Russell and Bromley shoes and handbag, and a posh hairdo, she went into Yates's on Oldham Street to meet her friend. I said to her, 'Right, it's 8.30. I'm going down to the club to make sure everything's OK. I'll send the car back for you at 9.00.'

Anyway 9.00pm came – and went – with no sign of either my mother or the car. At 10.30pm, I was standing on the steps of the club when she eventually walked in. On one hand, instead of the lovely leather handbag I'd bought her, was a plastic carrier bag. In the other was a tiny present wrapped in foil paper with a ribbon attached. Behind mother came Mary, carrying a jar of pickles in one hand and her sister Edith (who was a little worse for wear) in the other. I said, 'Mother, what on earth are you doing?'

Waving the carrier bag at me, she replied, 'Mary Barrow's done me some sandwiches.'

I said, 'But we're having a buffet!'

She said, 'How did I know? You never said.'

I was a bit angry now and said, 'Of course you knew. I do a party for you every year and I've got all these people here.' I then noticed her feet; she was barefoot. I said, 'Where's your shoes?'

She smiled and said, 'In the bag with the sandwiches.'

We finally got her smartened up and, as she went into the club, everyone sang 'Happy Birthday' to her. The place was full of flowers and it was lovely night and she loved it, although, if she had had her own way, she'd have preferred to have stayed in Yates's with her friends. Like I said before, you could never change Mum.

To me, Mum was my whole life; I absolutely lived and breathed her. She didn't want for anything and I clothed and fed her and made sure she had the best of everything all the time. Towards the end of her days, she developed lung cancer and spent a while in hospital trying her utmost to fight it.

Eventually, she did seem to make a slight recovery and I decided to take her out of the hospital and nurse her myself at home. Unfortunately, she had a relapse not long afterwards and I had no alternative but to call an ambulance. She died in the BUPA hospital in Whalley Range on 27 May 1995 at the age of 77, and a part of me died with her. She wasn't a smoker in later life, but had been in her early days.

I was absolutely devastated and in no fit state to do a thing. Fortunately for me, my manager Michael Ryan was on hand and I asked him to make the funeral arrangements on my behalf. Billy had been in touch with Michael Kennedy's Funeral Directors on Oldham Road, and I finally plucked up the courage to go and see Mum for one last time as she lay there in the Chapel of Rest. Perhaps my biggest regret in life is the fact that I never really told her just how much I loved her. Because I was always doing this show or that show, going here, there and everywhere and trying to make my name, I never seemed to find the time. Now, of course, I never could.

Susie Mathis and Sue Johnston were among the literally hundreds of people wanting to pay their respects to Mum. So many turned out for Mum's funeral that Michael had to arrange for a police escort as we took her to her final resting place in Gorton Cemetery to be alongside Dad. I think we had about ten funeral cars in the cortège with countless others following behind. In the same week we buried Mum, Michael's dad was also diagnosed with cancer, so it wasn't the best of times for any of us.

The day of the funeral itself was a Friday, normally a day the club opens, and I was obviously a bit uncertain as to what to do. There was a mass at St Anne's Church in Ancoats before we went to Gorton, and then we all went back to Billy Green's in Collyhurst for the reception and to give her a good send-off. At about 5.00pm, I said to Michael, 'Come on, it's time to go to work.'

Before the show started, I took hold of the mike and told the audience that I'd buried my mum that morning and then dedicated the first song to her. When I'd finished, the whole house gave me a standing ovation for which I was truly grateful. I did the show and tried as best I could to work it off, if you like, but deep down I was still devastated. I think what got me through the night was the fact that I knew that was what Mum would have wanted.

The day after the funeral, I went back to the little bungalow I'd bought her and I stayed in it on my own for about six weeks. My whole world was shattered and I was so depressed it actually made me ill. In the end, I tried to pull myself together and decided to put the bungalow up for sale. I put the boards up on a Monday and by the Friday it had been sold. I think it was the best thing I could have done, because had I not sold the place I'm convinced I would have had a nervous breakdown just leaving things as they were. Even though I had a place of my own, I just buried myself totally in the bungalow. Apart from the bungalow itself, I also found myself with lots of time on my hands, time I'd never had before, and the whole situation made me brood all the more.

When Mum died I was living in Shuttleworth and my daily routine just fell apart. With Mum around, my routine had been: up in the morning, in my car, down to Mum's. Pick her up and take her to the market or wherever she wanted to go shopping. Go to my office and make sure a cab was ordered to collect Mum and take her home. Back to Mum's every night for my tea before going home. At home about 8.30ish, I'd ring her to see if she was OK and wanted to go out for a drink. If the answer was 'Yes', I'd drive back again and give her a lift to Billy Green's. This was every single day without fail.

When she died, it gave me so much free time and I didn't know what it was. It took me years finally to come to terms with it. Seven months after I'd sold the bungalow, I found myself back in the little cul-de-sac, parked outside the house. Then it dawned on me. 'What are you doing here?' I asked myself. It was so routine to me, it was almost like being on automatic pilot.

Mum's death was undoubtedly the worst time of my life, as well as being the emptiest. Not only had I lost my mother, I'd also lost my best friend. I was glad she'd been able to have all the things I'd given her, and I was also glad she'd been able to see me at the height of my career. I was so sorry that Dad had died much earlier, because I know I could have given them a wonderful life together.

All these memories of Mum have taken us on a bit of a detour – but back to my charity work.

Pendlebury Children's Hospital in Salford is another cause very close to my heart and has been for the last 20 years or so. I said I'd try and help in any way I could and was invited, as a patron, to go along and look at the cancer ward. When I saw the ward and the kids in it, I thought, Bloody hell, I just couldn't believe the conditions they were putting up with. At the time, they were trying to raise enough money to buy a £1.5 million scanner and had about £800,000 in the kitty when the late Dr Jaffe, then chairman of the committee, retired and I took over the chair.

I think the very first fund-raising event I did for Pendlebury when I was chairman was back in 1992. I remember holding an auction at the Cocotoo Restaurant on Whitworth Street for, of all things, celebrity odd socks! We had one from Muhammad Ali and another from John Major, and it's perhaps the most unusual auction I've ever presided over. Pete Waterman joined myself, Susie Mathis and Bryan Robson and we raised more than £20,000 on the night.

If that was the most unusual charity event I've been involved with, then perhaps the most dangerous thing I've ever done for charity is a parachute jump. I did it one day from a small propeller plane over Barton Aerodrome in Eccles. There was a picture of me in the papers soon afterwards and the caption read 'Foo Foo Lammar gets in her plane'. After this people were coming up to me saying, 'I didn't know you had a plane, Frank.' I've *never* had a plane; lots of cars, yes, but never a plane.

Through work I'd already done with some of the Manchester United players, I managed to persuade the then captain Bryan Robson to get involved with Pendlebury. He joined me as joint chairman and between us we raised the missing £700,000 and put the scanner in. The final act in raising the money took place in March 1994 at a celebrity auction at Manchester Town Hall. We needed to raise just over £25,000 and, with the help of actor Ian McShane (from *Lovejoy*), and what seemed like a never-ending stream of Manchester United players past and present, we finally reached our target. In fact, we actually beat it by more than £5,000. Amongst the prizes sold on the night were an Eric Cantona original painting, one of Mick Hucknall's jackets and a fabulous day's shoot for eight people at the Duke of Westminster's Estate in Northumberland. It was a great feeling to be able to say that the necessary equipment had finally been ordered.

After that, I decided that it was about time the entire ward – The Beauchard Ward – was rebuilt and, with Bryan having moved up to Middlesbrough, I set about raising the necessary money – all £500,000 of it. This we named the Mend a Broken Wing Appeal. The old ward was so antiquated, all people could do was sit around the beds and the whole thing was very depressing. I decided they needed play areas, a computer room and proper lounge facilities and rest rooms for parents who needed to stay overnight. I also built a bone marrow unit for the poor children who can't take the chemotherapy.

When all this building work was completed, Sir Alex Ferguson officially opened the new ward. By this time, we'd become very good friends and when I asked him if he'd perform this opening ceremony, he was delighted and agreed immediately, although he did have one slight concern. The date I wanted him in Pendlebury coincided with him being in Paris commentating on the World Cup. In the end, Alex told me not to worry and, true to his word, he was there, right on time, on the day. What I didn't know until the day itself was that Alex had flown in especially from Paris for the ceremony and then he immediately flew back again to honour his television commitments. This, for me, tells you everything about one of the most generous men I know, and I can honestly say I feel very proud to class him as one of my greatest friends.

One particular fund-raising show we did in September 1994 still stands out in my mind. My good friend Dougie Flood at Quaffers in Bredbury kindly allowed us the use of the club facilities for a Sixties night. Mike Sweeney and The Thunderbirds, Wayne Fontana, The Dakotas, Peter Sarstedt and Susie Mathis, together with The Paper Dolls, all gave their services free for what turned out to be a fantastic night. The raffle prizes were not to be sniffed at, either. We had holidays in Florida and Portugal, but the star prize was a bright red Triumph TR7 that had been presented to former Manchester United star Jimmy Greenhoff after he'd been named Man of the Match in the 1977 FA Cup Final.

Another night I remember (again with Susie) was at the famous Yang Sing restaurant on Princess Street in Manchester. They were celebrating their tenth anniversary at that address and kindly offered the proceeds of the night towards the Broken Wing appeal. If memory serves, I think we came away that night with something like £4,000.

In my photo albums at home, I've got some lovely pictures of kids taken at Pendlebury in the 1970s and '80s whilst undergoing chemotherapy. I'm delighted to say many of these managed to pull through and are now adults; indeed, some are married and now have kids of their own. To this day, they still tell me they remember me visiting them in the hospital, taking them presents and just trying to cheer them up. It's a lovely feeling for me when some of them say I was the best medicine they got. Simply via bums on seats, I was in a better position than most to raise the money for this charity. I had no idea at the time just what effect my efforts would have on the lives of these children. Just to see their faces light up is reward enough for me to keep doing it for as long as possible.

Although there are many, many successes, there are also, of course, some regrettable failures. I'm sorry to say some children are not as fortunate as others and fail to make it, despite all the care, attention and medicine given and, at times, it can be very traumatic. One positive aspect that often comes out of such awful times is the number of distraught parents who put all their problems behind them and become voluntary workers for the charity.

I get lots of letters about my charity work and the majority of them ask me the same question: 'Why haven't you been knighted or OBE'd?' I always give them the same answer – truthfully, I have been ... inside my own heart. I know what I've done, I've done for the people who needed it and not for any sort of reward or title. Anyway, I think the real reason why they've not honoured me is because they don't know whether to make me a Sir or a Dame! Seriously, though, because I started with nothing from 'the land of the flying piss-pots', I decided that the most genuine thing to do was to put something back into society. The public made both Foo and Frank and this is my way of repaying them. Although I don't do my charity work for any personal recognition, I do have to admit to feeling very proud one day in December 1998 when I was named Celebrity of Commitment by the Manchester-based organisation Community Leisure Projects.

Top boy band Take That were big friends of mine and the Pendlebury Children's Hospital. Before they became massive stars, they even rehearsed once during the day in a completely empty Foo Foo's Palace. Imagine if I was to say now Robbie Williams was playing Foo Foo's tomorrow night; I don't think the place would be empty then! Later, when they played to a packed GMEX Centre, they gave me a cheque for nearly £90,000 for the hospital. I know the boys and their former manager Nigel Martin Smith very well and it was lovely gesture from all of them.

In the spring of 1983, I tried to raise some money for one particular young lady with no connection at all to Pendlebury. I found out about a 16-year-old schoolgirl called Lisa from Droylsden, Manchester, who was apparently allergic to everything and spent her whole time sneezing. It was costing her nearly £100 a day for a private hospital room in London and she still had to sleep on the floor because she was allergic to the bed. At first, I couldn't decide what to do, until one day I stumbled across the perfect solution that not only would help Lisa, but would also satisfy a need I'd had for a long time.

I was having my car cleaned near to the Apollo Theatre on Ardwick Green when I just glanced up at the hoarding outside the theatre. I can't remember the name of the group who were playing, but right across the poster was a huge sign saying 'SOLD OUT'. It got me thinking, I've never heard of them. If someone I've never heard of can sell out the Apollo, then surely Foo Foo Lammar can do the same. I wondered how it all worked. So, on the spur of the moment, I went straight into the theatre to ask them.

The outcome of the meeting was that I hired the Apollo for one night and got a dancing troupe together with the late Brian Fitzgerald and the 29-piece Northern Dance Orchestra and we did *Foo Foo Lammar in Concert*. The show on 31 July 1983 cost me nearly £25,000 to stage and was worth every penny. I described it at the time as 'three hours of pure filth'. The place was packed with about 3,000 people; it was a complete sell-out. Staff at the Apollo said they couldn't remember tickets for any event selling so quickly. At the end of the show, some of the regulars from Mum's local, Billy Green's, made their way to the front of the stage and presented me – dressed in a brand-new, specially made diamante cape – with a lovely floral arrangement … in a 'gazzunda' – a piss-pot! After everything had been totted up, I'd managed to raise almost £10,000 for Lisa.

Another local hospital I've supported many times is the Manchester Royal Infirmary. One memorable occasion, in particular, took place over Christmas 1986. The hospital was desperate to buy new, state-of-the-art cancer-beating laser machines. The only thing holding them back was the small matter of £100,000, which the NHS simply didn't have to give them. So we set about raising the money. I organised a £2-a-ticket night at Foo Foo's that included a raffle with the first prize being the opportunity to take a trip in a hot-air balloon. I'd have liked to have won that myself, although some people might say that as I've already got enough hot air to fill a balloon, there was nothing stopping me from going whenever I wanted!

That same year, I was very honoured when it was suggested I might receive the Freedom of Manchester for all my charity work. My name was put forward by Marlene Starr, otherwise known as Countess Miglioli, husband of Italian Count Bruno Miglioli. At the time, Marlene ran a jewellery shop in Hale and I felt very proud when I heard the news, although in the end nothing ever came of it. Marlene had worked out that, in the previous 12 months, I'd raised over £1 million for various Manchester charities and was even quoted as saying, 'He's done more for Manchester than anybody else,' which I thought in itself was a lovely thing to say. For a while, I was quite looking forward to being 'a lady Freeman' and although Marlene had canvassed a variety of councillors for their support, I'm still waiting. But, right from the outset, and everyone who knows me will confirm this, I've never done charity work to benefit Frank Pearson. I do it purely to benefit those who find themselves in a less fortunate position than me.

Pity, though, it would be nice to park the Rolls anywhere I like without having to worry about traffic wardens.

5

Sweet Charity

$\mathcal{I}$ CAN'T STRESS ENOUGH that in the early days – the 1930s and 1940s – we really never had the proverbial 'two ha'pennies to rub together'. Although times were undoubtedly tough, in all honesty I couldn't describe them as traumatic; in fact, I have to say that, largely, my life has been a pretty good and fortunate one. One day in 1986, though, very nearly changed my life for good.

I had a letter from the Inland Revenue saying that they wanted to see me in their Manchester offices. So I kept the appointment – well, it would have been rude not to – and they told me they 'believed' I had a bank account in my name and another one in my mother's. On top of that, they 'believed' I had one on the Isle of Man and a fourth in Jersey.

Immediately, I cleared things up. 'Yes, that's right,' I told them. I told them the truth because, as far as I was concerned, as I'd made all the arrangements with my usual bankers NatWest, I'd done nothing wrong. There was certainly nothing devious in it.

As for the money I made in all my other jobs outside Foo Foo's, I just paid it into the bank and basically just left it there. That was it as far as I was concerned; I never really thought about it any further. All the money from Foo Foo's Palace was paid in; proper books and the like were kept and the club paid the income tax. As for the other earnings over the years, I felt that I wasn't trying to hide it, especially as it was paid into accounts using my real name and not someone else's or even a bogus one. Despite all my pleadings with them, it was no good. In the end the taxman took £760,000 from me. I left his office, went into Henry's by the side of Kendal's on Deansgate and had a brandy and ginger ale. I did a charity show the same night and forgot about it. At least, as well as you can forget losing more than three-quarters of a million pounds! On top of all that, I then had to pay the VAT on it as well as a few other penalties, but I blame nobody but myself. It was all my own fault. I had to work like buggery for a long time afterwards trying to pay it back but, in the end, I did clear it all up. Interestingly enough, though, the Inland Revenue did actually recommend a good accountant who would certainly make sure this kind of thing didn't happen again. His name was Chris Gumley, so I rang him up and, some 16 years later, he is still my accountant.

For me, the worst thing about this was not the money. It was

Mum. I know if she'd have found out about any of it, she would have worried herself sick and I couldn't bear that. I got myself so wound up about this that I telephoned Susie Mathis while she was on air one morning at BBC GMR and asked to meet her. We met for lunch at the Four Seasons Hotel near the airport and tried as best we could to come up with some kind of strategy. This proved to be more difficult than either of us thought, so we arranged to go back for dinner to the same hotel the next night. By the time 4.00 in the morning had arrived, the liquor trolley had been completely emptied and I can't remember either now or then what we decided upon, if indeed we decided on anything. For some terrible and unknown reason, I felt I was still sober enough to try and drive home. I managed somehow to get out of the car park and on to the motorway where, after about 200 yards, even I knew enough was enough. I pulled on to the hard shoulder, switched off the engine and collapsed into a deep sleep.

The story about the money never really came out in public. If I'd have done what Ken Dodd did and gone to court with it, everyone would have known about it and I still would have had to pay it back. I couldn't see the point in that. I suppose someone must have let the taxman know, but I wasn't looking for any kind of revenge. I'd done wrong and was just glad to get it all over with. The whole incident didn't stop my earning power. I knew deep down that I would eventually regain the money I'd lost, so I just carried on as normal and, despite the obvious strain of such a loss, I began to look at ways of buying more property.

I sold my investment in Napoleon's and then, towards the

end of 1987, I bought Brubaker's on Portland Street and reopened it as Adam's. Once again, we had a big celebrity opening with all my *Coronation Street* star friends, as well as Bonnie Langford and Dora Bryan, turning out in force.

I was also involved in a place called Hippo's in Middleton, a club that was memorable if not least for its magnificent light show and a 20ft-high catwalk that housed the DJs. A story in the newspaper picked up on the apparent disappearance of Helen Worth and her husband, television actor Michael Angelis, from the opening night bash. It was the only slight sour note on an otherwise terrific evening and it's a shame the many good things weren't mentioned. But that's what happens when you're in the public eye as much as I am; you have to take the rough with the smooth. I think at the time (spring 1988), Hippo's was the fifth club I owned.

In more recent times (November 1994, I think it was), I bought Metz on Brazil Street in the village. This was a joint venture with Colin Rigby, and is a place, for those who don't know it, that stands right along the riverside. For our first anniversary party, I invited all my friends from Manchester United and *Coronation Street*, but our plans to hold this on the floating barge outside were scuppered when work on the new roof hadn't been completed.

But before Metz, again with Colin Rigby, I bought a sauna – Unit One – on Fennel Street near the Cathedral.

Obviously, a sauna is a bit different from a nightclub and I didn't know a great deal about how to run one. Unit One had 29 bedrooms (if that's the right word) and had been a gay sauna for a good few years before we took it over. Although it did good business, for us it was a relatively short-lived venture. We had some office space in the basement and I remember going to the sauna one afternoon to catch up on a bit of paperwork only to see the police carrying out some mattresses. I said to one of them, 'What are you doing with those?'

He replied, 'We're looking for semen.'

I said, 'I think you're a bit late; the seamen have already left.'

There was one particular policeman who seemed to have it in for us. He'd got it into his mind that we were running some kind of knocking shop and believed there were all sorts of sordid goings on. For all I knew, there probably were in the bedrooms but, then again, the same could be said of any 'decent' hotel anywhere in the country. He said that innocent people could wander in off the street, expecting to find a straight sauna, only to be converted instantly into gays. Anyone with any common sense at all had to spend ten seconds at the most inside the place to work out exactly what it was. There was never any trouble at all; people who had innocently made a mistake could leave freely without any interference from the staff or customers. We were all convinced the policeman was wrong, but he stuck to his guns and produced a case strong enough to take to the Crown Court.

It was an expensive day for me. We lost the case and £10,000 into the bargain. We could have appealed but decided not to in the end. I don't like any kind of trouble with the police and certainly don't like my name splashed across the papers for this kind of thing, so, after a while I decided to sell it on. I think the policeman in question has since left the force.

It wasn't the first time I'd appeared in court, although the previous occasion, I'm delighted to say, didn't cost me a penny. I'd taken some of my staff from The Picador out for a meal to the Piccadilly Indian Restaurant, which is still there today, right at the side of the train station. We found ourselves seated close to the serving hatch and when it was open we could see most of the kitchen as well as the staff. One kitchen worker decided he'd have a bit of fun and started to flick some chips through the opening at me. I let this go on for a while and then I leant through the hatch and dragged him across the table before hitting him in the face with a bowl of hot curry. He took me to court over the incident and actually had the cheek to say, in court, that the reason I'd attacked him was because I fancied him and he wouldn't return my advances. It was complete fabrication; I didn't even know his name. Fortunately, the court believed me this time and I got off.

Despite the problems with the sauna, I've always been on the look-out for ways to increase my property portfolio – or look at new buildings to buy, whichever way you want to say it! In the past, I almost bought Placemate 7 on Whitworth Street but, owing to a misunderstanding, I lost out on that one to Brian Lucas, my old partner from The Picador days. I was all set to spend £250,000 and wanted to make it *the* place in Manchester where any visiting actors or theatricals could go after their shows had finished. But, in the end, it wasn't to be; it was a fantastic idea, though. At one point, I even thought about buying The Talk of the North in Eccles from Joe Pullan, but when I worked out just how much money I'd need to spend on it, that was the end of that.

Not long after I missed out on Placemate 7, I was also unlucky when my plans to buy the old fire station on London Road collapsed. I had big plans for that place; I was going to turn it into a really upmarket club and would limit the membership to a certain number of very select people. Even though that building is still empty today – some 15 years or so after I became interested – it didn't stop me looking at property in the same area.

In more recent times, I moved into Monroe's Hotel on the opposite corner, where I have a room upstairs. My niece Debbie (brother Tommy's daughter) and her husband Michael (my manager) are the actual proprietors; I just get in the way, eat and drink and help out behind the bar occasionally.

While the investigation into the sauna was going on, I decided it was time to move house again. I'd changed from Failsworth a few years earlier, living for a while on the same street (Hardfield Road) as Colin Crompton in Alkrington, near Middleton, just around the corner from another great comedian and good friend of mine, Bernard Manning. After that, I bought an old farmhouse in New Moston and then, in 1988, moved to another farm, Highfold Farm, this time high up in the hills in a little place called Shuttleworth, near Ramsbottom.

Before I took residence in Shuttleworth, there was a story going round that I was moving in next to Bryan Robson and his wife in Hale. This was pure speculation, even though a story did appear in the newspapers. It all came about one summer's day when I was standing outside Bryan's house with his wife Denise and we were looking at the house next-door which was at the time up for sale. Someone happened to be driving by armed with a camera (I still don't know who), snapped a photograph and, before you knew it, two and two were making five and I was moving in. Just as I supposedly owned my own plane, the story was complete fiction; all we were doing was looking at the house like most people do when they know one's for sale.

I'm sure the locals in Shuttleworth thought aliens had landed the day I moved in! I don't think they'd ever seen anyone quite like me before. It was a beautiful, isolated place complete with six bedrooms and its own wrought-iron gates and indoor swimming pool. I love being around people, but the beauty of Shuttleworth was that it gave me the opportunity to be able to find a little bit of privacy when I needed it. Built originally in the eighteenth century, the house also had a conservatory, a sunken bath and converted barn. I changed the old snooker room into my bedroom and, although it was by far the biggest house I'd ever owned, I made sure it had all my bits and pieces in it to make it both warm and welcoming. Over the years I was there, I loved to throw lavish dinner parties, but I left the cooking side of things to John Nottingham who also worked for Kendal's. Despite my efforts with the fire and mop buckets at The Picador, I still struggle to boil an egg properly! Alex Ferguson and his wife Cath were regular visitors, as were *Brookside*'s Sue Johnston, Barbara Windsor, Les Dawson and, of course, Liz Dawn.

I got it for what I thought was a bargain – £165,000. About seven acres of land came with the house and it gave me the opportunity to keep a white Alsatian bitch (Zimba), two

Bichon Frises (Fluffy and Duffy) and a couple of Boxer dogs, Zara and her son Rocky. I'd always liked dogs from when I was a youngster but, living in Ancoats, we had neither the money nor the space to look after them properly. I was given the Bichon Frises by a couple of friends who were emigrating and was asked by a charity if I'd take Zimba because she'd had been neglected by her previous owners. The dogs used to get plenty of exercise up on the hills, but they were also quite partial to travelling around in the back of the Rolls occasionally. As well as being good companions for me, they were also excellent guard dogs.

Unfortunately, I lost Zimba when she slipped out of my property and killed a sheep in a neighbouring farm. Tommy Taylor, the farmer, shot and killed her and, although I didn't blame him in the slightest, it was a very sad time for me. I didn't fall out with Tommy about the incident – after all, it was his livelihood – but I never ate lamb chops again afterwards! Fluffy had escaped with Zimba through a gap in the fence and was also shot by Tommy. He was hit very badly in the leg and I spent £2,000 on operations for him. At the time, it was felt that if he survived at all, he'd never walk again but, eventually, he managed to pull through and was fine again as time went on. On top of the £2,000 for the operations, I had to spend about the same again to have the property refenced. My manager Michael Ryan said, 'All that money and you haven't even seen a leg of lamb.' How sympathetic!

I had Zimba buried with 'full honours' and when the man from the pet cemetery rang me to ask if it was a burial or cremation, I told him, 'Oh we can't have her cremated; we're

Catholic.' When a third member of the Boxer family came along in the summer of 1993, I christened her Sophie and I've still got her today.

I really did love living in the little village of Shuttleworth with its population of around 1,000. Some of the shops up there were wonderful, not least the 'chippy' and the wine shop, and I'll never forget Olive from the cake shop who made the finest vanilla slices and meat pies you could ever wish to taste. Not surprisingly, everyone in the village knew me (and my FOO 1 licence plate) and even though it is a small place sometimes it would take hours for me to do my shopping because everyone liked to stop for a chat. Like I said, though, I loved every minute of my time up there (and the people) and wouldn't swap it for anything.

I spent about 12 years in Shuttleworth before moving back to Manchester, and nowadays I divide my time between a flat at the Piccadilly Basin and a room above Monroe's. I got £450,000 for the farm when I sold it, so as well as giving me some wonderful memories, it also gave me a nice return on my initial outlay.

Granada did one of their *Lifestyle* shows from the farm and I let my very good friend Liz Dawn (Vera Duckworth from *Coronation Street*) shoot some scenes there when she made her video. I've known Liz for more years than either of us cares to remember and, like me, she started her career as a pub singer so knows exactly what I've been through. Again, like me, Liz does a lot of charity work – especially for breast cancer – and I help her occasionally and then the next time she'll help me with one of my causes. She's been to Foo Foo's many, many times and when she's had a couple of drinks, I'll get her up on stage to 'do a bit'.

I must say, though, that pleasure is not restricted solely to Liz. It goes for anyone famous who comes in the club. In the past, I've also managed to persuade Joe Longthorne and Roy 'Chubby' Brown to make an appearance. I class Roy as a dear friend and offstage he is nothing like he is on it. He was with us for New Year once when I'd taken Mum off to Tenerife, and about ten of us went out for a Chinese meal one evening. I insisted on paying and when the waiter arrived with the bill I gave him my credit card. A few minutes later, he came back. 'Card no good,' he said. 'No money.'

'Of course it's good,' I said, snatching it back from him, 'Give it here.' It turned out he was right. By accident, I'd given him my Asda petrol card by mistake! I felt such a berk but everyone else, especially Roy, thought it was hilarious.

Liz Dawn particularly loved my kitchen and asked if she could do some filming in it, so naturally I said 'Yes'. Just to confirm there were no ill feelings between us, Paul O'Grady was also a guest that day. And while we're on the subject of *Coronation Street*, I'm delighted to be able to say that I'm good friends with most of the current cast, as well as lots of stars no longer in the show, or sadly with us. One of these was the great Pat Phoenix who played Elsie Tanner for many years and I've actually still got one of Pat's fur coats in the dressing room at the club. I let her use the stage at Foo Foo's to rehearse a play she was going to appear in in Manchester shortly before she died. In the mid 1980s, I did quite a bit of fund-raising with Pat when she was involved in her famous Buy a Brick appeal.

I can remember opening Debenham's newly furnished cosmetics department one night when we raised over £1,000 for her cause.

Liz Dawn has been to more than one party at the house I owned in Shuttleworth. Sometimes, these could only be described as 'crazy' when my guests just got wilder and wilder as the night went on. I can still see Les Dawson on all fours doing a dog impression! On another occasion, Liz was sitting having a conversation with Les when a man entered the room and some of the other guests began to nod and say, 'Look who's just walked in.'

Liz turned to Les and said, 'Who's that fella then?'

Les said, 'That's Harold Riley.'

Still none the wiser, Liz said, 'Who? I've never heard of him.'

Les told her, 'He's a famous painter. He's the bloke who painted Manchester Opera House.'

It was then that Liz said – and this is the God's honest truth, you couldn't make it up – 'What, on his own!'

Les explained that he wasn't that sort of painter, only for Liz to reply, 'Oh, right. I thought when you said it, he'd be bloody tired doing it all by himself.' I'm sure Liz had a vision of Harold stuck at the top of a ladder in his overalls.

The producers of *Coronation Street* once asked if they could use Foo Foo's as the setting for a factory girls' night out. Of course, they really went to town trying to make the place look a lot more down-market than it really is, filling it with drunks and what have you, and they even had their own smoke-making machine. I think the scene was for a hen night for Bet Lynch (Julie Goodyear) and I can also remember Ivy Tilsley

(Lynne Perrie) having to cope with the attentions of a drunken admirer. However, the most memorable bit for me was seeing Vera Duckworth wearing a bright yellow party dress with shocking pink tights – an outfit not even I would wear!

It was even rumoured once that when Bet left the street in 1995, I would take over from her behind the bar in The Rovers. Unfortunately, it was all paper talk, although I must admit, I would have loved the opportunity to have worked alongside her, even if had been for just a few episodes. Can you imagine Bet and Foo behind that bar? No prizes for who'd have the biggest earrings, though!

Another dear friend was Jill Summers who played the man-eating Phyllis Pearce on the *Street*. Jill was a real lady and a very comical one as well. She lived in Osset in Yorkshire and was married to a very eminent doctor. Not unlike myself, she could easily switch on the airs and graces and would regularly come out with, 'Oh, hello. How har you?' as if she was born into the aristocracy. She and her husband would often come around for a meal and, in her posh voice, she'd say, 'Do you know, this is wonderful, isn't it?' She would then turn her face to the side and say in her famous gravel voice, 'It's better than a bit of dick.' Jill was a real character; a lovely person.

During a break in filming the *Lifestyle* programme, I can remember one of the crew from Granada saying to me, 'You've got a lovely place here; can we have a look at your dressing room?'

I was a bit confused. 'What dressing room?'

'You know,' he said, 'The one where you keep all your frocks.'

'Ah, no,' I said. 'You're getting me mixed up with Foo Foo. She lives at the Palace; Frank lives here. There's no frocks here.'

Another story related to this house came from my mother. It concerns the first time she saw the place. I'd picked her up in the Rolls and was driving up to the gates when I pressed a little handset inside the car and the gates opened automatically in front of us. Mum never said a word, but it impressed me! When we got to the house, I got out and (the proud son) said, 'What do you think then, Mum?'

She gave the place a good going over and replied, 'You'll never get a window cleaner all the way out here.'

Like I keep saying, Mum was Mum and it took an awful lot to impress her. I think deep down inside, though, she was quite pleased with what I'd achieved. I think she especially liked it when I met royalty.

On the same day Her Majesty the Queen opened the magnificent Lowry Centre in April 2000; she also attended the nearby Red Cross building, where I was fortunate enough not only to be a guest, but also to have the opportunity to meet her personally.

During the time we were fund-raising for the scanner at Pendlebury Children's Hospital, we had a visit from Princess Anne. Of course, she didn't come on her own; not only were the local and national press there, but also the international press. Bonnie Langford was also with us, along with some local radio presenters, many of our helpers and Bryan Robson. It was planned for Princess Anne to meet everybody one at a time – a bit like they do after a Royal Variety show – so we all made a nice straight line in one of the hospital corridors for her to walk along. She must have been told that the first person she was going to meet was Bryan Robson. What she didn't know, however, was that Bryan had swapped places with me; I was to be the first one introduced. So I'm standing there all suited up and she comes in, shakes my hand and says, 'Mr Robson, I believe.'

'Oh no, Ma'am,' I replied, looking at Bryan. 'He shoots, I only dribble. I don't play football.'

She was a bit taken aback and then saw my little lapel brooch that read 'Mr Lammar', and asked, 'What do you do then, Mr Lammar?'

'I wear frocks, Ma'am,' I said truthfully.

She managed a polite little giggle and a slightly confused, 'Oh really?'

I went on to say, 'You're a Princess, Ma'am – with respect, I'm a Queen!'

I was hoping to have a little chat with her about women's fashion, but the mix-up took the wind out of my sails a bit. Of course, all the cameras flashed and the papers were full of headlines like FOO FOILS ANNE the next day. But I have to say that she took it all in good spirit and proved to be a lovely person. She stayed for something like two-and-a-half hours and we even had a cup of tea together afterwards. Looking back over the years at all the famous people I've met, Princess Anne is probably the one who has impressed me the most.

When we got the recognition for the work done at Pendlebury with a royal visit, it made me feel very proud. Not only for myself but also for the generosity of the Mancunian public for helping us to achieve our goals. I've always said that every little helps towards this cause and one such example occurred around Christmas 1987. The landlady of the Hat and Feathers pub on Mason Street in Ancoats (Carole, along with her husband, landlord Ian) had thrown open their pub for a charity night and booked several artistes, including myself. However, on the night itself, the majority of them (mentioning no names) failed to turn up and I had to spend most of the night on stage on my own. It was very hard work but, in the end, we raised more than £700 so all the effort was worth it. Carole was very complimentary about me in the papers the next day, which I thought was a lovely thing for her to do.

The Night of a Hundred Men was another show I staged to try and help Pendlebury. The name of the show described it perfectly. Everyone on stage at the Apollo was male, whilst everyone in the audience was female. I presented and produced the show that was billed as 'naughty but nice' and featured footballers, actors and some huge burly strippers and we raised about £30,000.

I've been very fortunate through my charity work to have met a lot of the Royal Family, from the Duchess of Kent to Princess Diana. The first time I had any dealings with Diana came about through Jason Turner, one of the helpers who works in the charity offices. Jason had read in the papers about Diana recently auctioning off about 80 of her ballgowns at a charity bash in New York. One day, out of the blue he said to me, 'I'm going to write to Princess Diana. She seems a very generous woman so I'm going to ask her if she'll donate something for us to auction.' We were all delighted a couple of weeks later when we got a lovely letter back from her along with a silver and enamel trinket box, the kind of thing you'd use on a bedroom dressing table, which went for £6,500 at a celebrity auction held at Manchester Town Hall. This was a wonderful night for us when more than £55,000 was raised. Shortly after the auction, I then received a personal cheque from her for £500 to go towards the fund-raising. I was completely stunned (and that takes a lot, believe me) when she replied and everyone connected with the charity was absolutely thrilled by her generosity.

Although I have rubbed shoulders with royalty, I have also, on occasion, crossed paths with some people you certainly wouldn't invite to a posh garden party. In 1996, not too long after my mum had died, I did a show for Liz Dawn's breast cancer charity at the Regiment pub on Hulme Hall Road in Salford – admittedly, not one of showbiz's top venues, but nevertheless a gig – and it was for a good cause.

I was on stage as the lovely Foo in all her refinery (long black dress and blonde wig) when a heckler started having a go at me from the side of the stage. Well, normally I love this. If they heckle me during the show, it's almost like my party piece. I know how to handle them and can turn the tables easily when I have a go back. But this guy in particular was proving too much. He was a huge man, about 6ft 3in with a ponytail and covered in so many tattoos he looked like a roll of cheap wallpaper. I didn't know his name at the time, but when the story came out in the papers the next day, he was described as 39-year-old Rick Lynch from Moss Side. Apparently, he'd gone there to sing in the talent show.

When I do the shows as Foo, my hands are covered in rings. However, none of them are worth more than a couple of quid; I never wear the 'good stuff' on stage. This fella said something about my not being able to wait until my mother had gone so I could get my hands on her rings, and I just snapped. I lost it completely. I went over to the side of the stage and smacked him unmercifully with a beauty straight in the face. Not a sequin moved; not a diamond dropped. I was very proud of the shot. When he got up, I hit him again, this time with a lovely right hook to the mouth. He must have seen me as an easy target, standing there in a frock, but he obviously didn't know about all my experience as a boxer in my younger days.

My immediate reaction was to look down at my hand and check my nails were intact. That would have been terrible, because I had another show to do immediately afterwards! Fortunately, everything was OK and, although I could easily have done without the incident, I wasn't in the least bit sorry for what I'd done. As far as I was concerned, he'd got exactly what he deserved.

The next day, he took the press back to the pub to show them where this giant of man, built like a brick wall, had been smacked by a drag act. He was obviously hoping to make a few bob out of it and, who knows, maybe that was his intention all along. When the police found out about the incident, they more or less told him he got what was coming to him (which he had done) and suggested he 'moved on' and forgot about it. I've still got the cutting from the *Manchester Evening News* (dated 23 January 1996) describing the incident. In it, the licensee of the pub, Angela Creeley, is quoted as saying, 'I've banned Mr Lynch from here. He was barracking Frank something rotten and his language was appalling. Frank was well within his rights to have a go back.'

People tend to forget that, even though I wear a frock a lot of the time, I was brought up to look after myself from day one. Remember, I'd also had some practice during my stints as a doorman at The Picador Club, so though I don't like to be rough, I know how to be when the time arises.

If you, the reader, are any good at sums, you'll have worked out (assuming, of course, you've also read page one of this book) that at the time of the incident at the Regiment I was 59 years old – or, to put it another way, 20 years older than Mr Lynch – which I think makes the whole thing even more remarkable.

This book is the first time I've ever admitted my true age. Although some people have known the truth for years (and have not been too ashamed to broadcast it), I, like many other celebrities, have always managed to shave a few years off here and there and generally tried to confuse as many as possible. In March 1997 I was the victim of a surprise (but nevertheless correct) sixtieth birthday party. Normally, people fail to keep secrets from me, but this time I never suspected a thing.

To celebrate my birthday (although I never said which one it was), Liz Dawn asked me to have a quiet drink with her at The Rovers Return on the set at the Granada Studios Tour. When I opened the door, I found myself confronted by about 100 family and friends who were all in on it. The place was packed with famous faces – Bryan Robson, Alex Ferguson, Susie Mathis, Les Dawson's widow Tracy and Manchester's senior police officer David Wilmot are just a few names I can remember. Also at the do was Louise Roberts, the lady who'd made my first frocks all those years ago. To cap it all off, Shirley Bassey impersonator Maxine Barrie leapt out of a huge cake and sang 'Happy Birthday' to me. It was a fabulous night, but I was adamant about the number of candles they'd put on the cake. I told them all they were wrong – 'I'm 50-something and not ready for my bus pass yet' – although I'm sure a lot of the guests there knew the truth. It does no harm to throw a veil of mystery over certain things, I always say!

6

Love, Love Me Do

$\mathcal{I}$T'S TO BE HOPED that the reader (in other words *you*) has not skipped the rest of the book and headed straight for this chapter in the hope of finding some smut. No doubt, you will find something of a sexual nature here, but go back to the start and read it from page one, you dirty little sod!

For most of my early days, I have to admit to not being sure whether I was 'Arthur or Martha'. I have had the occasional brief flirtation with girls, and have never tried to hide any of my true feelings but – and those who know me really well will confirm this – I am a very private person. Even today, you'll hardly ever see me around the village and you certainly won't see me doing my shopping wearing one of Foo's frocks. I wear the frocks because they are part of my persona; they are part of my act. Even though I will admit to wearing them (and feeling good in them), I don't wear them for any sexual gratification. There is a great distinction between Frank Pearson and Foo Foo Lammar. Over the years, I've turned down countless, really well-paid after-dinner speaking jobs. I'm always asked to do these as Foo Foo, in full drag, and every time I say 'No'. I consider wearing the frocks purely as a way of earning my living on stage. I won't stand up in front of 400 or so men, say a few words and then sit down again for the rest of the evening. I don't eat in drag and I don't take the drag home with me. Apart from just the once that is, when I was living in Shuttleworth and did a show nearby. I didn't see the point of getting changed at the venue after the show, as it was so close to home, so I drove home as Foo Foo. The bloody dogs went mad when they saw me coming through the front door because they didn't know who the hell I was! The very next day, all the drag went back to Dale Street where it's remained since.

With a large percentage of my friends and associates being 'celebrities' (footballers, television stars and the like), I have always led a very full life and no one questions my sexuality and anyone who knows me knows just who I am and what I am. When people see me with famous 'men' such as Ryan Giggs and Alex Ferguson, they can't believe that I am genuinely friends with these people. I'm sure they think that they are not my type of people and I just rub shoulders with them for publicity purposes. Let me say here and now that nothing is further from the truth, and I can give you one such example as proof.

I was on holiday in Marbella not too long ago when Ryan Giggs rang me to ask if I'd attend a function for his benefit year ... and attend the function as Foo Foo. Because Ryan is a friend, I was delighted to do this and flew back to Manchester for just the one night and then went back to Marbella. Ryan knows the difference between Frank and Foo and made his request (and his decision) based on what he knows. He felt that the function would be funnier if Foo attended rather than Frank, and so it proved. I know that the way I am with people – regardless of their sex or their preferences – I can earn their respect and they treat me accordingly.

Another story concerning Ryan and me found itself on the front page of the *News of the World* with the bizarre headline Ryan Fights for Drag Queen. Not for the first time in my life they'd got things out of all proportion.

I'd been invited by United to attend a celebratory party in recognition of their treble success in 1999. Not surprisingly, there was plenty of drink available and almost everyone there on the night got a bit merry. One man (the son of a very well-known figure at United who should have known better) was a bit worse for wear and said some uncomplimentary things to Ryan's mum. Ryan overheard these remarks and challenged him, a situation that only caused the man to turn on Ryan.

I was standing close by and heard and saw what was going on and so stepped in to try and calm things down. In footballing terms, it was 'handbags at ten paces', but unfortunately a journalist spotted it and the next morning it was in the paper.

I think my profession is just like being a top electrician, top mechanic or whatever. Like me, these people want to do the job to the best of their abilities, but when they finish work, they can just forget it and go out and enjoy themselves. When you're in showbiz, in the public eye, it's very difficult to stop actually being at work, and sometimes I think people struggle to understand professionalism.

My brothers have never questioned my life. To this day, none of them – or my late mother for that matter – has ever asked me if I was gay or not. On my part, I've never discussed it with them, probably because I didn't think they'd understand even if I'd have tried to explain it anyway. Their wives and children all know about and accept me for what I am, but it's just something that's never arisen with my brothers. They've just got on with their own lives – Tommy in his coal business, Jimmy who spent many years in the building trade before becoming a full-time carer for his tragically wheelchair-bound wife Bernadette, and Brian, who took early retirement from ICI after a heart scare and now earns a bit of money as a part-time chauffeur.

I suppose it's a sad thing, really, but I put at least some of it down to me never seeming to find the time to stop and tell them. Whatever my sexual preferences, when I was diagnosed as having cancer (which, by the way, is not unusual on my dad's side of the family), everything was put into its proper context.

When I opened The Picador Club back in 1971, I was living in a two-up, two-down house on Mount Street, just behind the Prince of Wales pub, an area long since replaced by the Mancunian Way. How shall I put it? 'Keeping me company' in that house was a Liverpool lad called Tommy Doyle. I can still remember Tommy in the passenger seat of the powder-blue Zephyr I was driving at the time. Tommy used to own a poodle and would generally look after me and did my washing at the nearby laundrette. He'd march off down the road with his poodle under one arm and my washing under the other, and would sit gladly for what seemed like hours in the laundrette chatting to the other women in there.

As well as washing, he was also a dab hand in the kitchen. On one Sunday, I'd stayed late in the Prince of Wales after a lunchtime show and was just having a quiet drink behind closed doors with some of the staff. I'd lost track of the time completely and had forgotten about the roast lunch Tommy was preparing at home. Mind you, *he* hadn't. He came storming into the pub absolutely livid and in front of everyone hit me on the top of the head with a plateful of food. It looked like something out of an old slapstick movie with the gravy and peas running down my shirt collar. We were together for about two years or so before we separated although we remained on friendly terms and I do still bump into him occasionally whilst shopping in town. Tommy is a similar age to me and I think he has recently retired after working for the Ford Motor Company for a long time.

Before I harboured any thoughts of what you might call a steady relationship, I have to admit to having more than the occasional one-night stand. In the late 1950s and early 1960s, Piccadilly Gardens was a wide-open space and on Friday and Saturday nights the whole area around Queen Victoria's statue was packed with hundreds and hundreds of people. Some were staying at what was the Queen's Hotel on the corner of Portland Street; some were just out for a breather from one of the many nearby pubs; and some were out simply for sex. Because of this, not surprisingly, there were plenty of other people more than willing to help and, I have to admit, occasionally, I was one of them.

Along with a couple of friends, I used to go regularly, in full drag, in the hope I'd pick up. Not far away from the Gardens was an area (ironically around Dale Street and Hilton Street) of open space that long-distance lorry drivers used for their overnight stops. Far away from home, these drivers would then venture down into Piccadilly to see what was on offer, although some of them got a lot more than they bargained for when they got me, I can tell you! The more experienced among us told me, 'Never get in the lorry with them. Always give them a wank or a blow-job at the side of the cab and make sure you get the money first and shove it down your underwear.' More happy days!

One such day, though, wasn't particularly happy. I took notice of the advice given to me about staying outside the cab and, as this bloke was adjusting himself after the event, his wallet fell out of his pocket and landed near my feet. While he was busy getting himself dressed, I picked the wallet up and began to walk away from him. Unfortunately for me, I hadn't got too far when he noticed it was missing. He came running after me swinging a bloody starting handle and hit me hard across the top of the head with it. I was in a right mess with blood everywhere and had to go to Ancoats

Hospital (still in full drag, mind you) where they patched me up with four stitches.

Another time 'on the Dilly', I was stopped by a policeman who started to ask me questions. It was a summer's evening and I can remember to this day exactly what I was wearing. A black skirt, red fitted blouse, stockings (complete with a black seam running up the back of the leg), suspenders and stiletto shoes. No wig was needed then as I had my own long, wavy hair. His first question was, 'How old are you?'

'18,' I replied.

'Where do you live?'

'23 Butterworth Street, Bradford, Manchester,' I replied again.

'Mother's name?'

'Leah.'

'Father's?'

'Charles,' I told him.

'And where's he?'

'He's in prison,' was my honest reply.

When he asked me the next question I wasn't as honest.

'And what's your name?' he asked.

Thinking quickly on my feet, I told him, 'Winifred,' after my mother's middle name.

He didn't for a minute believe me and said, 'Well, Winifred, do you know what I'm going to do?'

I thought I knew but said 'No'.

He continued, 'I'm going to give you the chance of your life.'

'How's that?' I asked.

The policeman smiled at me and said, 'Because I'm going to kick you right up the arse if you don't get into that cab and get home and get your fucking jeans on!' He pushed me towards this taxi and I took his advice – at least for the time being. I know I was lucky, but back then everyone did exactly as they were told when the police spoke. If they said 'Jump', you jumped or you ran the risk of a thick ear, something I think would not go amiss nowadays.

A familiar sight (along with the boys and girls) in Piccadilly Gardens were the mobile stalls which traders used to set up every night selling a whole manner of things such as hot-dogs, pies, tea and coffee. One Saturday night, Rusty King and I visited one of these stalls and Rusty had a hot-dog whilst I had a meat-and-potato pie with gravy.

As we were just leaving the stall after I'd paid, a great big fella muscled his way in between us and demanded from the owner, 'Ten Park Drive.' He looked annoyed to say the least, and the dried blood coming from his nose and resting on his top lip indicated he'd been on the wrong end of a good hiding not too long ago. The owner handed over the cigarettes only for this man to try and do a runner without paying for them. Well, the owner, a woman, still on the other side of the stall, wasn't having any of this and she grabbed him by the hair and tried to pull him back. As she was pulling one way and he was pulling the other, the whole cart started rocking backwards and forwards and in the commotion, my red blouse copped all the meat pie and gravy. Rusty ended up flat on the floor minus his hot-dog and every pie on the stall fell off and finished up a useless pile on the floor. The woman must have lost all that night's profits with the pies going all over the place, but she was determined she wasn't going to let go of his hair until he'd paid for the cigarettes.

When the police arrived, they carted the fella off straight away but could only look on in amazement as I was just sat on my arse on the pavement, in full drag, covered in bloody pie and gravy! I've had a lot of laughs in Piccadilly Gardens.

Nowadays, of course, this area has been altered almost beyond recognition. In those days, it seemed like everyone there was shagging. That's all that ever went on, with the prostitutes and whoever they'd picked up constantly at it on the wooden park benches. It was an unbelievable place.

Lewis's Arcade about 50 yards away was another place that almost rivalled the Gardens. Even the hundreds of pigeons in the rafters didn't prevent the young (and not so young) from having a good time, providing, of course, you could stand up for long enough!

My first serious and long-term relationship was with a man called Alan Owen. I first met him in The Rockingham Club in the 1960s and although I was about ten years older than him, we seemed to hit it off immediately. Up until that point I really didn't know which way I was going. I'd worked constantly with women, whether it be at Lawson's or Butterworth's or in the pubs and clubs, and loved being around them.

I told Alan from the start that I was a nightclub singer and arranged to meet him for our first date at The Grand Hotel on Aytoun Street. What I failed to tell him was just exactly what kind of a singer and performer I was! The plan was, I'd pick him up and then he'd watch my show afterwards.

I pulled up outside the hotel, once again in one of Butterworth's lorries and I was in full drag, complete with wig, pencil skirt and high heels. After causing much merriment and consternation amongst both the hotel staff and customers, I managed carefully to get myself out of the cab and marched into the hotel. I'd arranged to meet Alan in the bar, but at first I couldn't find him. I had no option but to shout at the top of my voice, 'Where's my baby, where's my baby?'

Everyone, including a most surprised Alan, looked round and nobody could quite believe their eyes. Then I spotted him. 'Come on, come on, we're off to the gig,' I told him and, with Alan's mouth still gaping open, we left the hotel together. I drove the lorry up to Belle Vue with Alan, dressed in his best suit, in the passenger seat. Not surprisingly we got a few strange looks from other drivers as we headed up Hyde Road.

We stayed together for many years, lived together at the bungalow in Failsworth, and Alan later managed The Picador Club for me. We gradually drifted apart with no animosity on either side and today, although we don't see each other nearly as much as we used to, we still remain good friends. In fact, Alan worked for a while at Metz until I sold my interest in it early in 2002.

Today, I'm happy to say that after the best part of 30 years, I'm still with Billy Hughes. The Pearsons and the Hughes families have known each other since Billy's brothers and mine palled out together in their younger days. People who know me well will tell you that I'm really a very private person. People who know Billy will tell you he's even more private than I am. Between us, we like to keep ourselves to ourselves and we hope that, as we don't bother anyone, then they won't bother us. That, for me, is a major strength in the relationship and, as it's worked for so long, we have no plans to change it.

7

Foo Wheel Drive

*A*S MENTIONED ELSEWHERE in this book, I've had a constant supply of pets throughout my life. Probably not too far behind the number of animals I've looked after is the number of cars I've owned.

From my very first van – the Ellis's meat pie van all those years ago – through to the Rolls-Royce I drive today, I've always had a passion for motorcars. Perhaps this passion comes from my days in Ancoats when there was never any chance of any of the family ever being able to afford to buy one and now I'm just trying to make up for it. Who knows? I'm certainly not going to try and analyse the fact and neither will the car dealers of Manchester!

I think most people know by now that my first vehicle was

a former Ellis's meat pie van. Once that had finally passed on, my attentions turned to a second-hand Ford Corsair. The third car I owned was also the first new one I ever owned. I bought a beautiful, powder-blue Ford Zephyr from Manchester Garages on Oxford Road. I loved the colour – blue car to match my blue eyes! – and really just bought it because I wanted to be seen around town in it. It was easily the biggest car I'd owned up to then and, to be honest, I didn't realise just how big it was. I'd only had it four days when I misjudged its length and hit a milk float trying to overtake it. The bonnet was covered in eggs, milk and all sorts. The milkman, too, was less than pleased with me! God knows what was going through my mind because milk floats only travel at around 10mph! Even today, people are still astounded when I tell them I managed to hit one.

As I got on at work, I was granted the privilege of being given a company car. Even though it was undoubtedly a privilege, at first it was a bit of a come down for me. I sold the Zephyr only to receive a Ford Popular from the firm! That was replaced by a Vauxhall and I had a company car every year from then on until I left in 1971, so I shouldn't really complain.

I think it must have been some time in the early 1980s (when I'd begun to earn good money from the clubs) that I really went to town and bought a red Ferrari Testarossa. I remember buying it from Bauer Millet on a Monday and taking it back on the Thursday. Even though it looked great and was a superb car, I couldn't get in and out of the thing. It was like driving a snuffbox! I could only just about get in it with my own hair and knew I had no chance when I had Foo Foo's wig on.

Even though I only had the Ferrari for four days, it still lasted longer than some pillar-box-red Asian Range Rover-type thing I bought. That lasted just two days! When I got in it, the seats adjusted automatically and it felt as though I was going up and down in a lift, so it had to go.

Of all the cars I've bought over the years, I've never test-driven any of them; I just buy them for the colour. Some you win, some you lose.

I've simply lost count of the number of cars I've owned over the years, but as for Rolls-Royces alone, I think ten would be a conservative figure. The first one of those was the old Silver Shadow model. Of those ten, unfortunately two have been written off.

A collision I had on the corner of Oldham Street and Lever Street in April 1999 almost wrote me off as well. It was broad daylight and I was driving along minding my own business when a red Volkswagen Golf pulled across and collided with the passenger side of my light-blue Silver Spirit II. I later discovered that another car had pulled out from Stevenson Square right in front of the Volkswagen, forcing it, in turn, to hit me. The Rolls seemed to bounce off the Volkswagen, demolished a set of railings and then ploughed into a clothes shop. The shop itself was situated right on a corner and it was this 90° angle that gouged a huge 'V' in the front of the car, completely demolishing all the headlights and radiator and forcing the bonnet upwards, completely covering the windscreen. The car was eventually towed away but was found to be beyond repair, and so I had no option but to get another one. As for me, I was slumped against the steering wheel with my face covered in blood. The two women in the Volkswagen managed to get me out of the car and sat me down on some office steps until the ambulance arrived and took me to Manchester Royal Infirmary. I had stitches in a gash over my left eye and across the bridge of my nose, and for several days afterwards, as the bruising and swelling came out, I looked like the loser in a heavyweight boxing match.

Almost as familiar on the streets as my face is my personalised number plate, FOO 1, and this came about purely by accident. I think it must have been just at the end of the 1970s and I was driving along one day on the way to Blackpool (in the Silver Shadow I think) to see Shirley Bassey in concert at the Opera House when I found myself behind a really clapped-out, four-door Rover saloon. The only good thing about this car was its number plate – FOO 1 – and I knew immediately I just had to have it. Before I could speak to its owner, I'd lost the car in traffic, but was determined not to give up on it so I began to make some enquiries. Eventually, with the help of a solicitor, I tracked the owner down in St Anne's and bought the car (including the plate, which was all I really wanted) for £600. The car was probably worth about £30 but to me the number plate was priceless. When I offered the owner £600 he said, 'You're doing yourself, lad. The car's not worth that much.' I knew full well it wasn't, but felt that the plate would bring me a lot of good luck, and so it's proved. In the end, I managed to sell the car for £300 so the plate itself actually cost me £300. Not a bad buy when you think that I later turned down an offer of £25,000 for it from a Chinese gentleman. I wonder what Foo means in Chinese? Or maybe it was just his name. It's become a travelling advert for me and, ever since then, it's been on whichever car I've owned, apart from a very short time while I had to have some new ones fitted.

Some local wag had spotted my car parked in town and decided to have a bit of fun. Armed with a brush and some black paint, he altered the plate (very professionally, actually) to read FOO L and I drove around the streets of Manchester for a couple of hours completely oblivious until someone stopped me and told me about it.

I've also been known to own a car that, at least luxury-wise, is not in the same class as a Rolls or Bentley. I once owned a yellow Pontiac sports car – complete with gull wings, I think they're called. Instead of the doors opening at the side like they do on a traditional car, these opened on the top like something out of *Star Wars*. One particular night, I was driving up Rochdale Road after a show with Michael Ryan and Geoff Reeves as passengers, when I fell asleep at the wheel. Michael (in the back) still remembers the car veering across to the right-hand side of the road, but I made light of it at the time. I told them, 'I wasn't asleep; I was just resting my eyes.'

Michael was furious saying, 'You're not supposed to rest your bloody eyes when you're driving.'

Curiously, Geoff (who was a real character and well known for playing tricks on me and lots of other people) never said a word, as though everything was quite normal. I had to get rid of the car eventually, because it wouldn't handle the hills outside the farmhouse.

Because of my charity work at Pendlebury Children's Hospital, I've spent many hours driving up and down The Crescent in Salford. A lot of this time was admittedly faster than the law allows, and I got stopped by the police for speeding on more than one occasion. I was finally banned for 12 months but carried on driving and, sure enough, got stopped again and they served another 12-month ban on me.

Once again, I ignored it and once again they caught me. This time, though, instead of another ban, I had to make an appearance at Salford Magistrate's Court. When I got to court, I was amazed at the number of different charities that had turned out to give evidence on my behalf. Everything they said about the good work I did and the fact that I couldn't do as much without the car was all true but, despite all their efforts, I was still fined £700. It taught me a lesson and I never speeded again after that.

If I can't remember the number of times I've been stopped for speeding, then who knows the number of parking tickets I've had! It's a pity I never enquired about a possible partnership with the company that prints the tickets. I suppose, really, it's just something that comes with the job. I've always been flying around all the over the place doing various shows, and sometimes I just had to leave the car wherever there was a space.

I do have to say, though, that because of the number plate, people do recognise the car and can usually work out where I am nearby and what I'm doing. There are a lot of wardens today who respect me for what I do and try to find me and suggest I put another pound in the meter fairly quickly. They certainly don't come down on me as hard as they used to a few years back.

8

Talking Frankly

*W*ELL, NOT COMPLETELY FRANKLY ... even I have to have some privacy!

Over the years, people have asked me the same kind of questions – 'What's your favourite ...' 'Do you like ...' and so on, so what I thought I'd do is get them all down on paper (at least those I can remember) and probe myself in print!

What's your favourite holiday destination?
Holidays for me really started when I got into showbusiness and began to earn a few bob. We never had what you might call holidays in my younger days. I'd say that probably from my mid-20s onwards, I've tried to make up for it.

Of course, before you can travel abroad, you need a valid

passport. A few years ago, I booked a holiday only to notice afterwards that my passport had expired. When I filled in the forms to order a replacement, I altered my age slightly – nothing too drastic, I just shaved a few years off. I sat back to await the arrival of a new passport and received an official envelope from Liverpool some weeks later. Instead of a new passport, the envelope contained an even more official letter asking me to call in and see them at the time shown. It was obvious from the tone of the letter that some eagle-eyed civil servant had noticed my slight alteration.

I kept the appointment expecting the worst, but when the stern-looking clerk saw my face, his tone changed alarmingly.

'You're Foo Foo Lammar, aren't you?' he very nearly screamed at me. When I said 'Yes', he said, 'Oh, please come down to the door at the end and I'll let you in.' So I went and he did.

He then screamed again to all the girls in his inner sanctum, 'I've got Foo Foo Lammar here. Come over and meet him.' So they all did and we spent a few minutes chatting with me, signing autographs and posing for a few photos. Fortunately for me, the male clerk was a 'friend of Dorothy's'. His actual words to me were, 'Oh, we won't worry about your age.' I left Liverpool about half-an-hour later with a brand-new passport!

One of my favourite places is Tenerife and every Easter I used to take Mum and her friend Dulla there for a few days. I knew a lot of people there and we'd meet up regularly with some friends including Roy 'Chubby' Brown and the singer Brenda Law.

I can remember one trip to Tenerife when I stopped a game of bingo literally dead in its tracks. I'd gone with my good friends Sheena Busby (the late Sir Matt's daughter) and Arlene Brown, the widow of David Brown, the man responsible for first importing the Proton car to Britain. The three of us were out one evening for a stroll when we walked past a roadside bar that was holding a game of bingo. I heard the announcer say, 'Legs eleven,' followed by, 'Foo Foo Lammar!' He stopped the game immediately and came running through the crowd towards me and gave me the microphone. The next thing I knew, I was up on stage doing an impromptu five-minute spot. Even though I was ill with the 'flu at the time, I still did this little show because it felt so good that I'd been recognised all these miles from home.

Another reason, I suppose, is the fact that the announcer and the audience all felt as though they knew me personally and just assumed I would do it, which, of course, is absolutely right, I always do!

In the late '60s and early '70s, I became one of a 'gang' of about 15 or so who would have two weeks of summer sun every year in Spain. Some of the 'rogues' who came with me included Tony Marsden, Vinnie Morgan, Pete Ford, Tom Hampson, Les Bailey and Alfie Solomon, who not only seemed to be the ringleader, but was also the one constantly armed with a camera. We were in right at the beginning of the booming package holiday industry and became quite familiar faces in places such as Benidorm and Sitges. I'm sure I'm forever remembered at the Sitges Park Hotel, which was right in the centre of town and must have had something like 300 bedrooms. I had the place turned upside down with all the men dressed as women and the women dressed as men. They didn't know what day it was. I earned such a reputation that people from other hotels used to come to ours just to see me. Every night, I'd perform free of charge in the hotel ballroom where everyone (including the staff and management, who were no doubt grateful for the increase in bar turnover) loved me, so much so that when our two weeks were over, they carried me out of the hotel like an ancient god on some kind of wooden platform thing covered with flowers.

As the years went by, I had quite a few people coming up to me in the club who said they'd seen me in the hotel and commented on how good a time they'd had. It really was a good holiday. Everything seemed to go well and everyone in the hotel got on with everyone else and mixed together as though they'd known each other for years.

During the breaks from my unexpected but nevertheless enjoyable cabaret spots, we used to have the occasional day trip away from Sitges itself. One of these included a donkey trek high up into the hills where lunch had been laid on at a remote restaurant. It was the sort of trip you see on all the holiday programmes on television; about 15 donkeys in a line all carrying pale and frightened tourists with the lead donkey being pulled on a rope by a bored-looking Spaniard. The idea sounded good at first, but after we'd eaten, Tony Marsden and I were fed up with the whole thing and decided we wanted to get back to the hotel a bit quicker than was planned. So we left the restaurant, unhitched two donkeys from the trees outside and, after a little persuasion (and some bread), set off back down the hill. On the way back down, I said to Tony, 'I don't remember these little huts.' He agreed with me, but it was hardly surprising in the end when we found out we were going in the wrong direction. The donkeys definitely had minds of their own and, instead of taking us back down to the hotel, they decided they wanted to go back to their stables and to see their friends and relatives. Whatever we tried did not deter them from their plan. When we got to the stables the smell of what looked like tons of shit gave us a souvenir we both could have lived without!

Apart from Spain, there are, of course, the more faraway and exotic places I've visited. One particular trip in the late 1970s took me to Canada at the request of Marion Thomas, the former head cashier at Butterworth's Paper Mill, and her husband John, who'd emigrated there. The occasion was the wedding of their daughter Lorraine and so I went with my friend, Billy Hughes, to Toronto.

I'll never forget the trip we took to Niagara Falls. We went right down to the bottom of the Falls on a boat, covered from head to toe with hats, coats and wellies, and we still got bloody drenched. I can remember getting off the boat after the trip and a couple of other tourists recognised me and asked if I'd have a photograph taken with them. As usual, I said 'Yes', and just as I turned around to get into position, I fell off the boat and into the water. Fortunately, the boat was moored to the dockside and although everyone (including me!) panicked, they managed quickly to drag me (so to speak) back on to the boat and safety. If I was wet already from the spray and mist of the Falls, now I was completely soaked. Fortunately, the other people reacted immediately, or else Foo Foo Lammar would have been the latest to have gone over Niagara Falls with not a barrel in sight! Even though I looked liked a drenched kipper, the people still wanted their photograph.

I can honestly say that wherever I go (and don't get me wrong here, this is not a criticism) people constantly ask for me to pose for photographs. This is something I'm always delighted to do, and the day they stop asking will be the day I'll start to worry! It's lovely to be recognised, no matter where I am, and I can even get stopped at Manchester Airport *before* I actually arrive on holiday. One year I caused such a crowd at the airport that I was asked by a member of British Airways staff if I'd like to move to their VIP lounge so they could get on with their job properly.

Another trip took me to St Lucia in the Windward Islands. It was especially memorable because while I was in the Caribbean, I found out that the holiday firm we'd booked with had gone bust and for a while no one knew just how we were all going to get back home. I'd gone with Colin Rigby and some of the locals told us about this lake thing deep in the forest that supposedly contained sulphur or some such thing and was great for the skin and complexion. So, naturally, we went to have a look.

In the end, we found something that could only be described as a 20ft-deep tub standing in a small clearing but with no sign of human life anywhere nearby. So we waited a while until two huge women arrived and we made some enquiries about the tub. They said we could use it and then they told us to strip off before they literally picked us up and threw us in. Every few minutes or so, the women would climb up the steps on the outside of the tub and start to slap us around with some bloody great palm leaves. I said to Colin it reminded me of a Palm Sunday that had gone horribly wrong! Whatever was in the water and the thrashing we got from the leaves certainly made us much more relaxed, and we both felt a lot calmer and generally better for the next few days. Of all the places I've been to, I think St Lucia is probably the most exotic.

Along with some other landlords and landladies – about 30 of us in total – I once took a 17-day cruise to the Caribbean on the *Canberra*. It was the first time any of us had ever been on a cruise and we had a fantastic time. All we did, all day, every day (apart from when the cabaret artist Joan Regan made me get up on stage) was eat and drink. We dressed formally for dinner every night and the food was so good I put on about a stone-and-a-half in 17 nights. I can't remember the exact date, but it must have been in the early 1970s and I think it cost around £500 for the trip, which was a lot of money in those days.

I also remember a fancy dress party on this cruise. With Colin alongside, we went as Bonnie (me) and Clyde (Colin). Even though I had The Picador Club at the time I still wasn't too well known and so I thought I'd see if I could get away with it. I borrowed a dress from another passenger and, in the end, we collected the first prize of £250 from a very surprised Captain. Mind you, I don't think it was just the Captain who was surprised. The whole ballroom was stunned when they first saw me! The £250 never reached England; what we didn't spend on booze on the ship we lost at its casino. The ship itself was so big, what with cinemas, show rooms, bars and the like, that without fail, every single night, I got lost trying to find my way back to my cabin. Mind you, it didn't help that I was pissed most nights!

Colin and I also ventured to Tunisia, this time with another friend of ours, Geoff Reeves. Geoff was a big club entrepreneur then, one of his places being The Northern Sporting Club. He was also suffering with cancer at the time, so Colin and I decided we'd take him away for a few days and give him a break. I can remember we'd had dinner one evening in the hotel and then moved over to the bar and sat ourselves down on three high bar stools. Geoff excused himself saying he wanted to go to the toilet, and while he was away we had a visit from a German guy who decided he'd take the empty stool. I said, 'Sorry, that stool's taken. My friend will be back in a moment.' He was adamant he was going to take the stool and I got a mouthful of German abuse for my trouble. So, in the end, I got off my stool and gave it to him – right across the head. It sent him flying across the bar. Unfortunately for me, the German fell into a perfectly innocent waiter who happened to be walking by carrying a trayful of drinks. The waiter was knocked into the corner of the bar and regrettably had his head cut open. The management quickly telephoned the police and, moments later, I found myself in the back of a Tunisian police van along with this German. We were taken to the nearest police station and put into separate cells overnight, prior to our trial the next day.

The worst part of all this, though, was the timing of the whole thing; I was locked up the night before we were due to fly back to Manchester. Colin and Geoff took the flight back, leaving me all alone except for two lovely female Thomson holiday reps who came to see me.

If memory serves, I also had some help from the British Consulate and then had my time in court. I was fined for damage to the property at the hotel, furniture and glasses mainly, but I forgot all about my troubles when I later heard that the German had been fined more than I had. I also had the pleasure of knowing that I hurt him when I hit him. No one gets a smack off Foo Foo Lammar without them knowing about it!

In Kenya – again with Billy – I stayed at The Mombassa Beach Hotel, a beautiful place and one of the best hotels in the country. This, too, was a brilliant holiday. We met a barrister and his wife in the hotel and, as the time went on, became friends and got on really well. The four of us were at the airport together coming back, when the officials searched us at Customs. I got stopped by a huge security guard who ran a metal detector all over me and then noticed I had a big bulge in my back pocket. It was just a wad of English money – about £3,000 in notes – but all of a sudden there was a great crowd of people around this guard and me and I'm sure they all thought he'd caught a drug-smuggler or something.

On the way out on the plane, I'd filled out some form or other and said that, between me and Billy, we were bringing around £1,000 into the country. I never counted it going in, actually, and I didn't think it was any of their business. Well, of course, when they found out I was apparently taking more out than I'd brought in, they became interested in me. They took our bags off the plane and carted us off to prison for an overnight stay.

The cell wasn't the greatest. It was full of cockroaches and the combined toilet and washing facilities were made up of a leaking copper pipe running down the wall. We also had to share with two men we later discovered were ivory smugglers. Despite all these obvious discomforts, I still managed to get some sleep, but Billy stayed up all night bashing the cockroaches with the sole of his shoe!

Again I got help from the British Consulate and told them exactly what had happened and just how much I actually had and how much I'd told them I had. I have to say it was a bit scary because all the locals seemed fascinated with my money and I'm sure some of them would have done almost anything to get at it had I not told the British Consulate.

The next day in court, I was fined £50 for this 'deception' but, of course, had to use some of the remaining money to buy two new flight tickets home. We got to the airport dishevelled, unshaven and looking more like two drug-smugglers than we had done previously, but never got stopped once!

Reading this it seems that everywhere I go I end up in jail and troubling the local British Consulate. This is obviously not the truth but it does appear to be something I've picked up that's not shown in the brochures.

Again with Colin Rigby and Geoff Reeves, I once ventured to Pattani in Thailand. It was only our second night there when we saw an advertisement for a local theatre showing *South Pacific*. We booked the tickets for the next night and while we were waiting for our taxi from the hotel to the theatre, we had a drink in the bar. We'd been there just a few minutes when one of the hotel staff came over and said, 'Your taxi's arrived, gentlemen.' So we finished the drinks and went outside, only to find a huge elephant waiting for us! The bloody thing was on its knees and we had to climb up its legs and on to its back. Then its handler – a little boy who could have been no more than ten – walked the thing (and us) through the streets to the theatre. When we saw the show, I had another shock; the entire cast were men, including the false tits and everything. So that was two shocks in the one evening, but there was more to come. After the show, we went into a nearby bar where I had far too many drinks but did manage to get acquainted with someone I thought was a member of the chorus line, still dressed in all the gear. Anyone who's ever been to Thailand will know immediately how friendly the locals are and this proved no exception so, after another couple of drinks, we went back to the hotel room together. However, when it came to getting undressed, I was horrified. It was a woman, a fact made perfectly plain when she took her knickers off! Here was me thinking I'd pulled this gorgeous-looking male dancer when, in effect, nothing was further from the truth. I told her in no uncertain terms that she was no good to me and sent her packing immediately.

Sex is a massive business in Thailand. Everywhere we went we were constantly stopped by people with offers of 'You want my mamma?' or 'You want my pappa?'

Later on that same trip, I did manage to find someone more suitable to my requirements, and yet, fate intervened again. I'd gone with a charming young man to a room in what turned out to be a brothel, although it was a peculiar one to me as it was built on wooden stilts. The rooms were divided only by thin pieces of bamboo or hessian, and you could hear and see everything that was going on; boys with boys, boys with girls, girls with girls, you name it.

Now the Thais were generally very concerned about their hygiene, so before we had sex I had to have a shower. Inside this tiny shower cubicle was a bottle of shampoo and, after I'd washed my hair, some of the soap got into my eyes. I left the cubicle with my eyes closed and stinging, searching for a towel, obviously not aware of what was going on underfoot. I soon found out, though! There was a little trapdoor in the floor and, of course, I fell straight through it, completely naked, and landed on two lesbians on the floor below who were well at it. I mustered as much dignity as I could, made my excuses and left fairly sharpish. I wouldn't have minded but I'd already paid for the knock-off and never got it!

In 2001, I bought a place of my own in the sun, in a place called Monte Pariso in Marbella. It's a two-bedroom apartment with access to a communal swimming pool and is the perfect place for me to go and unwind for a few days, although because of work commitments I haven't yet managed to get over there as much as I'd like. Ideally, I try go on a Sunday and return home the following Thursday or Friday, so it's also fair to say that I'm quite fond of Marbella as well.

Tell us about your holiday home.

When I had the cancer scare, I decided to take the doctor's advice and try to cut down on work and also to try and relax more generally. I was still living up in Shuttleworth in the big farmhouse but felt it was just too big, too much for me. So I sold that and bought a flat in Manchester and an apartment in Spain. After the operation, I spent a week in hospital, a week at home and then a month in the new place in Marbella.

I seriously considered retiring at the time because the kidney cancer really did frighten me. But then I thought if I've got somewhere to go, a place of my own in the sun, then the chances are I might get better quicker. By doing this, I could then come back to the colder Manchester weather and still be able to do my shows. I'd leave my manager Michael to make bookings where necessary in my absence, obviously still allowing me my rest, and the other perfect thing about Marbella is that it's only a two-and-a-half-hour direct flight from Manchester.

No question at all that Marbella itself is a beautiful place, a lot nicer, in my opinion, than Benidorm. If I have any criticism of it, though, after the full month I spent recovering, I was beginning to get very bored just sitting around doing nothing. I knew obviously that that was the whole idea of going in the first place, but if I was ever to go and live there longer, then I'd have to work or run a bar or something, because I'm sure I'd end up pulling my hair out with boredom. Having said all that, though, I have every intention of spending a lot more of my time out there in the future.

What's the most extravagant present you've ever bought anyone?
I think I would have to say my mother's diamond rings. Over
the years, I bought her five rings, each of which contained five
individual diamonds. I'd buy these for various birthdays or
Christmases and, after she died, I had them all made into one
large ring that I wear today on my little finger. Probably the
nicest present I ever bought was the house for Mum and Dad.
Even though it was only a little house and, in comparison, it
wasn't a great deal of money, it's probably the best one single
gift I've ever given anyone and it's certainly the one that gave
me most pleasure in the giving.

What's the best present you've ever received?
Although money never actually changed hands and therefore
it's of no material value, I think the best present I ever
received was when Mum and Dad got back together after all
the upsets they'd had over the years.

As for material things, I've received a few over the years that
perhaps are not worth a great deal financially, nevertheless
they are priceless to me just for the sentimental value.

I once received a set of pearls from Liz Hennings, the
landlady of the Crown on Ashton New Road, one of the
regular pubs I sang in. The pub wasn't doing too well at the
time and I know she had no money really to call her own.
When she gave me these pearls – they'd previously belonged
to her mother – I'm sure she didn't know their full value. They
were a beautiful set and I wore them for years afterwards. By
the time she died some years later, I'd become well established
and could afford to buy quite a bit of good-quality,

high-priced jewellery. One day, for insurance purposes, I took all my stuff to be valued. I also took Liz's pearls with me. To my absolute astonishment, they were valued at £700. Of course, had I known their true value I would certainly never have accepted them from her in the first place. When I think back to what Liz could have done with all that money all those years earlier, it makes me quite sad. I've still got those pearls today and would never sell them.

Out of all the gifts (not to mention the thousands of cards) I've received over the years, I think the best one has to be seeing the success of my club whether it be Foo Foo's Palace or, prior to that, The Picador Club. Invariably, I've had birthday parties in the club and to see my family and friends enjoying themselves and having such a good time makes all my hard work seem worthwhile and gives me a lovely feeling.

Do you have a hero or heroine?
One of my favourite people has to be Danny La Rue. When I first saw him on stage all those years ago, I was still very much learning the game, practising it, really. I was mesmerised by his performance, by the glamour, the sparkle and, perhaps most of all, by the sheer professionalism of the man. A wonderful performer as well as being a very genuine and nice man.

Another great favourite, and someone I was proud to call a good friend, was Les Dawson. Everybody knew Les as the brilliant stand-up comic he obviously was but he was also a brilliant writer and conversationalist. He was a very sharp man and one I thought could have done well on the *Brain of*

Britain quiz show. He really was a comic genius. One of his sayings, and this was well before he was famous, was, 'It's nice to be nice, but it's also nice to prove it.' It's something I've never forgotten and I like to think I've kept that thought with me over the years.

In recent times, say the last ten years or so, another hero of mine has been Sir Alex Ferguson. I don't mean Alex Ferguson the manager of Manchester United; I mean Alex Ferguson the man. The press hasn't really got to know what Alex does and what kind of a person he is apart from his footballing career. Never once in all the time I've known him has he ever said 'No' when I've asked him to help me with one of my charity commitments. Whenever I've requested his help, within reason – in fact, sometimes without reason – he's always been there with me, right up at the front, many times bringing his 'lads' along with him. I've lost track of the number of times he's allowed the players to leave training early and attend some function I was involved with.

One example of his generosity involved two little boys who shared not only the same birthday but also the same isolation ward at Pendlebury Children's Hospital. I said to Alex that it would really cheer these two boys up if some of the players could find a few minutes to come down and have a chat with them, even if it was only through the glass. I offered to go and pick them up from the training ground in my car and take them over to the hospital and then back again. Alex told me that wasn't necessary and that someone would be there. A few days later, Nicky Butt, Ryan Giggs, Paul Scholes and Teddy Sheringham all turned up en masse at the hospital. The doctors said to me that the boys seeing and talking to the players was better than any medicine they could ever prescribe.

During the time I was trying to get the scanner for the hospital, I used to host sportsmen's dinners and when I announced that Alex and a couple of current first-teamers from Old Trafford would be on the top table, the £50 tickets sold out every time within a matter of days. In turn, I try and help them on match days with the corporate side. Indeed, the players now ask me to travel with them on European trips and I've become a sort of mascot for them. I always stay with the players' wives and others in the VIP parties and am always looked after extremely well. I was looked after a bit too well when I flew to Tokyo with United for the World Club Championship in 1999.

We travelled first-class on British Airways, I think it was, and superb food and champagne was the order of the day. After we'd had the evening meal and watched the film, I was just settling down for a few hours' sleep when I felt a nudge in my ribs. I turned over to see Bob Kinnerlea, Phil Neville's father-in-law. Along with Ron Wood (the former owner of the Birthdays card shops and a good friend of Bryan Robson's), Bob suggested we went to the galley for a few more drinks. Bob closed the curtains behind us and we stood up for the remainder of the trip – all seven-and-a-half hours of it – drinking. The stewardesses were marvellous. They kept topping our drinks up and said, 'You'll be all right in here; no one will see you.' Eventually, they went to bed with the final words, 'Please keep the noise down now while we go to sleep.'

The next time we saw them, it was morning. The girls returned to the galley, saw us still standing (just!) and asked us to sit down now as they were about to prepare breakfast. Within half-an-hour we were being fed and the plane landed an hour or so later. It was a brilliant trip and one I'll never forget.

I'll also try and help the club or anyone connected with it when they do their charity work so I suppose it works both ways, which is exactly the way it should be. I must say here that neither side ever asks for personal gain. All funds raised from whatever we do go straight to the charity concerned.

It's a great thrill for me when they ask me to make the half-time draw on the pitch on match days. The cries of around 60,000 fans chanting, 'Ooh, aah, Frank Lammar,' at the tops of their voices gives me goose bumps every time. And that's just for Frank; just think what would happen if I did the draw as Foo!

For me, Alex Ferguson is a lovely, lovely man. When he was knighted for his services to and achievements in football, I was delighted for him. However, I would also like to see him knighted again for all the work he does away from football.

If they ever made a film of your life, who would you like to play you?
Shane Ritchie would be ideal. I've know him for a long time and don't think he's ever done drag, although I may be wrong there, but what I do know for sure is that he'd put his heart and soul into it. I think he's a very talented, funny man, who without question could certainly play a young Frank, the Frank maybe prior to Foo in her prime.

As for Foo in the later years, I think another Manchester lad, Ian McShane, would be ideal. He can sing and act and would be capable of being as outrageous and as outspoken as me, and I mean outspoken in the nicest, polite terms.

Would you ever consider leaving any of your organs to medical research?
I'm not sure there's much left that's any good for me to leave! I've already lost one kidney but I have still got all my own teeth and they're in good condition. They could have them, I suppose, once I've rattled, but they'd never get them out. In all seriousness, though, if there's anything left that is of use and would help someone else, then they're welcome to the lot.

Do you have any regrets?
Yes, and no. To date, I must say I've had a brilliant life, so what I'm going to say may or may not be a regret. People often ask me why I've not done more work on television. The simple answer is that I was born and bred a Mancunian who started out with nothing. As time went on and I built myself up, everything I earned, everything I owned, I appreciated because I'd done it. Foo Foo's Palace to me was like The Talk of the Town in London, simply because I'd built it. I wasn't just an act who appeared there occasionally; the club was mine, I owned it.

Because of the success of the club, the television people offered me work constantly, in all honesty too many times for me to remember. Unfortunately, a lot of this work was in London and it meant me being away from the club often for days at a time. I knew that without Foo Foo there, there would be no Foo Foo's Palace. I had to make the decision either to be nationally well known or satisfied and, in the end, I chose to be satisfied. As it happens, I've still managed to do some television work and, who knows, when I retire from Foo Foo's I may do some more.

Having said that, though, even now after all these years, I am still proud of the fact that Foo Foo's is always full. Audiences who've been in the club from 8.00pm are still on their feet at 2.00am the next morning and, but for the doorman standing at the side of the stage, some of the party-goers would be on stage with me. I'm not a popstar; I'm an entertainer who plays to audiences ranging from 18 to 80, sometimes even 90. Foo Foo's Palace is always full of people right across this age range.

For instance, with lots of the hen parties that come in, it's not unusual for the prospective bride to bring their mums and aunties with them. This, for me, is the ideal audience; the younger ones keep me young whilst the older ones keep me realistic. If I was asked tomorrow to perform a concert in front of six nuns, twelve priests and the cream of nobility, then it would not daunt me because I know I could do it.

I've always based my act around honest vulgarity. Sometimes in my show, I know I'm a little suggestive, but only in a comical way. Dressed as Foo I always try and meet the audience before the show actually starts. By doing this, I'm already interacting with them and lots of them comment on the fact that it's unusual for the star of the show to mix with the punters. I think this also puts any slightly nervous members of the audience at their ease and makes me a more friendly, less threatening figure.

So, in my usual roundabout way, I suppose I'm saying that I both regret and don't regret trying my luck in television in London. If I had, I might not have been so successful in my home city.

Have you ever had any serious illnesses?
When I was a child, I had the usual things like mumps, but the one I'll always remember involved bugs. For the younger reader (please ask a parent or grandparent for more details) I will recount a tale of pulling back the already tissue-like wallpaper only to find bugs and lice running up the plaster.

For us, this bug problem was particularly troublesome in the little room we rented in Ardwick. Because we had no money, Mum went down to the council or whoever it was and arranged for the whole room to be fumigated to try and stop it. The week after it was done, I contracted measles, although at the time I didn't realise it. I carried on going to school, and one day was called out to the front of the class by the teacher for something I'd done wrong. Nothing new there then! Immediately, she saw these red spots all over me. Pointing to them she said, 'What are all those?'

I replied, 'They're bugs.'

She was horrified. 'What do you mean, bugs?'

'Bugs at home, they've bitten me.'

The next thing I knew, they'd started an inquiry but, of course, by then all the bugs had gone and the spots genuinely were measles. Of course, I knew they hadn't bitten me, at least not that many, and just wanted to get the teacher at it.

I think it was round about 1977 when I had a lumbar puncture operation in St Joseph's Hospital. It wasn't a particularly pleasant experience but, like most things that have happened to me during my lifetime, I wasn't going to let it get the better of me. I had the operation on a Tuesday and was back at the club on the Friday. That's the way I've always been. Some people call it stubbornness, but I call it determination.

I had a much more serious illness in the late spring of 2001. I'd been to Munich to watch a European game with United when I developed severe chest pains. To be honest, I'd been having them for a few weeks prior to the trip, but they were nowhere near as bad so I just shrugged them off. While in Germany, the pains were so bad that I had to call for a doctor over there and was so ill on the plane coming back that they pushed me through the airport in a wheelchair.

When Billy telephoned Michael Ryan with the news, Michael knew immediately I was bad. Simply because I was never, ever ill, Michael knew it could be something serious so he rang Dr Hardy, made an appointment for me and I checked into the Alexandra Hospital on the Tuesday after the game for what I thought would be some standard X-rays. I had the X-rays but was told I was to have a full body scan and some blood tests a few days later. When they got the results back, they told me they'd found a tumour on one of my kidneys. Ironically, that very same night I'd agreed to perform at a charity dinner for Christie's Cancer Hospital being held at The Marriott Hotel in Worsley.

I must admit to feeling shocked and emotional at the dinner, but I still honoured my commitments. Michael Ryan accompanied me to the dinner just to keep a 'maternal' eye on me and he was absolutely staggered that I'd not backed down. So, too, was Wilf McGuinness, the former Manchester United player and manager, who was Master of Ceremonies. I told them both that if I wasn't out working somewhere, I'd just be sat on my own at home moping and worrying about it.

I was referred by Dr Hardy to see Mr Payne, a specialist cancer surgeon, in his rooms at Victoria Park, who told me that, at least as far as he could see at that moment, the cancer was confined to the kidney. He said I'd probably had it for about six months and it was the reason why, apart from the chest pains, I'd been feeling less than 100 per cent.

Over the next few days, I thought many times about my mum and my brother Tommy. Mum had died from lung cancer and Tommy had had a scare about 15 years previously and, not surprisingly, I did fear the worst. Interestingly enough, they could find nothing wrong with my chest (I'd actually had a chest X-ray as a matter of routine about six months before), but had it not been bothering me so much they would never have found the tumour on my kidney.

I knew surgery was needed and that I'd be out of action for a while, but had only one concern on my mind. I said to Michael, 'Make sure the club stays open.'

Quite how he would do this, of course, I had no idea, because obviously Foo Foo would not be around. But he did (he kept the music and dance elements and drafted in a couple of drag acts as my replacement) and, by all accounts, the customers still turned up at the club as booked. Michael told them all exactly what had happened and, apparently, most of them were more concerned about my health than missing out on my show. I've not had a chance to thank them for their kind thoughts up until now, so here's a huge thank you to everyone concerned. I also know from Michael just how hard the staff worked and pulled together during that time. Again, here's a huge thank you to each and every one.

The following Tuesday, I was back in hospital (this time the BUPA in Whalley Range) and the surgeons were taking the kidney out. When I came to after the operation, the plan was for me to go straight into intensive care but I wasn't having any of that. Billy and Michael spent the night in hospital with me for support, but the effects of the anaesthetic wearing off caused me to keep drifting in and out of consciousness, so I wasn't really aware they were there for most of the time. Apparently (so they tell me), I nodded off in mid-conversation with them at one point so they took the opportunity to pop outside for a cigarette, being away from my bedside for no more than five minutes at the most. When they returned, I was awake again and shouted, 'Where've you been? I've been on my own for four hours!' They soon put me right.

As I came round, I couldn't help but think about my beloved Boxer dog, Sophie, and began to ask, 'Where is she? Is she all right?'

Michael said something like, 'She's fine; she's in the playpen downstairs,' but I'm still not sure whether I believed him, although I accepted his answer anyway. He could have said, 'She's flying round the moon in a rocket,' and that, too, would have been all right for me. Apparently, I also telephoned Michael at 6.30 the following morning and told him I was ready to go home and for him to come and get me. Looking back, I'm sure I was nowhere near ready but, to tell you the truth, I don't even remember phoning him.

Not long after I had the operation for the kidney cancer, I got a phone call at Foo Foo's from May Bromley, a woman I knew probably 40 years ago. Back then, May was a prostitute and worked the area around Ardwick Green. Apart from her bright red hair (which gave her the obvious nickname 'Ginger Minge') she had what I suppose might be called a trademark; every time she was working, she used to wear a fox stole, complete with the fox's head. People used to say to her, 'I bet your fanny's full of freckles, like an Eccles cake.' To say she was a rum bugger would be an understatement. One of her regular places to pick up business was a pub called the Gog and Maygog on Downing Street and I used to follow May and her customers outside where she would give me the money for safe-keeping. It wasn't unknown for customers to 'do the business' and then give the poor girls a bashing so as to get their money back.

On one particular occasion, she gave me the £25 (which was a lot of money in those days) and then took the punter to the side of the canal to satisfy his needs. I stood on the bridge overlooking the canal and, within minutes, I saw May's fox stole floating down the canal. I immediately thought this bloke (I think he was a lorry driver) had battered her to death

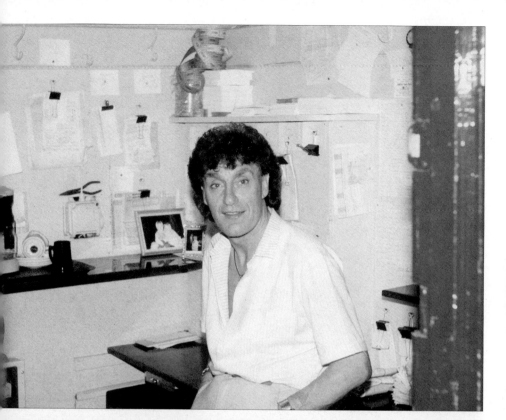

op: In the old office at Foo Foo's in 1983.

ottom: On stage at the Davenport Theatre in Stockport.

Top: At The Lightbowne Hotel in Moston, 1989. *Left to right*: Melvyn Taylor, me, Michael Ryan and Liz Dawn.

Bottom: With Sue Johnston from Brookside.

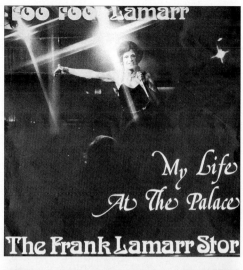

Top: My attempts to break into the charts.

Bottom left: With my very dear friend, TV presenter Susie Mathis.

Bottom right: With Jill Summers, aka Phyllis from Coronation Street.

Top left: Outside my house with my Rolls Royce in Shuttleworth.

Top right: With Mum at my 50th birthday at The Portland Hotel, March 1987. It's one of my favourite pictures.

Bottom: Liz Dawn and the late Les Dawson entertain my friends at one of the many parties I had in Shuttleworth.

Top: Billy Hughes and I in Marbella whilst I was recovering from my
cancer operation.

Bottom: Billy and I look back on some wonderful times at my 65th birthday.

©*Adrian Pope*

Top: On stage at Foo Foo's Palace with one of my many special guests. I can't remember this young man's name, but I remember it was his last night of freedom before joining the army. I hope he lasted longer than I did!

Bottom left: Staff from Foo Foo's enjoying a night out at the Palace in 1984.

Bottom right: With Billy in drag for charity, at Manchester Town Hall.

Top: The Queen and I, Salford 1999 and *bottom*, with the Duke of Edinburgh.

Stepping out with Sir Alex Ferguson, January 2002. ©Eamonn Clar

and then, for good measure, thrown her in the canal. I rushed to the nearest telephone box and called 999 and, within minutes, there were police vans all over the place. The police rushed under the bridge expecting to find God knows what, but they must have had a shock when they found May completely naked with this bloke giving her one. As if losing the stole and the embarrassment of it all wasn't enough, poor May was also fined by the police.

The six weeks after the operation were spent recuperating, but, for me, this part was worse than both the scare and the operation itself; I was desperate to get back on stage again. I was told the operation had been a success and I could continue to lead an ordinary life. I'm still on medication and go back regularly for check-ups and, apart from one minor scare in February 2002, everything (touch wood) seems to be all right.

After spending four weeks in Marbella, I felt really good and couldn't wait to get back to as much work as I'd been used to up to then. On my first night back Michael tried to talk me into easing my way into things by suggesting I did only the one spot instead of my usual three but – and not for the first time in my life, I took no notice of anyone but myself – I did the three spots; nearly two hours in total. Looking back, perhaps I did rush things and returned a bit too early.

Just before Christmas 2001 I went to Christie's for a routine check-up and scan only to be told that a small number of very minute particles, cells, had reappeared and spread to my lungs. Once again, I was immediately on red alert. Professor Hawkins (who, by the way, was very, very good and honest with me) told me that even though it wasn't curable, it was treatable. Straight away, he put me on a drug called Interferon, which by all accounts has had some good results so far, and it's hoped that this drug coupled with my immune system will get rid of these little cells. The first injection I had made me feel absolutely terrible but, as time has gone on, the more I seem to have got used to it, and I look and feel better than I have done for some time. I've been told that I could easily live for another 20 years or so if I keep up with the treatment, so here's hoping. I'm determined to fight this for as long as I can, whatever happens. I love my work and my life far too much to give into it easily.

Even though I have spent many, many days in and around hospitals because of my charity work over the years, it was only when I was diagnosed with cancer of the kidney that I truly realised just how hard the staff in these places actually work. The support I got from everyone I came into contact with, whether it be doctors, nurses, surgeons, specialists, BUPA, Christie's or whatever, was absolutely magnificent and I'd just like to put on record my appreciation of their efforts. Even though I'm still not 100 per cent over the illness, I know for certain that I'm in the best possible hands.

Because of the success and popularity of the club for more than 20 years, I think I can say without being too big-headed that I'm well liked by a lot of people. However, it was only when the story broke in the papers about the kidney that I knew just how well liked I was. In the weeks that followed, I got 1,600 'Get Well Soon' and 'Best Wishes' cards from people all over the country. I know this figure is accurate because I made a special effort to count them all. It was just the same with the flowers; I got so many that my private ward was completely filled and the staff had to move the overflow to the other wards. Through the pages of this book, I'd like to thank each and every one of you for taking the time to write to me and for those good wishes.

Another minor ailment that sometimes affects me is conjunctivitis in my right eye. This flared up again at more or the less the same time they discovered the cells on my lungs, so I decided just to get on the plane and spend a couple of weeks in Tenerife taking in plenty of sun and doing nothing at all.

The whole episode was not a pleasant experience and one I don't wish to repeat.

When I look back today and think, Would I have done anything differently or better with my life? I think largely the answer would be 'no'. I don't think I could have done any more good for sick people and for the charities I've been involved with. I think I could have, perhaps, paid more attention to me personally and given more love to my immediate family – including my 17 nephews and nieces – but, then again, I don't know whether that's true, either. Hopefully, I've got a good few years left in me yet to make these slight alterations.

Have you ever had any accidents?
Bloody hell, it's a wonder I'm still in one piece! I've had more accidents than the Bionic Man! I once had an accident in a show I was doing at The Offerton Palace in Stockport. The

owner had seen me working at a charity show and asked me if I'd do a spot at his place, one which unusually (as far as I was concerned) had a sunken stage. When the acts were announced over the speakers, the stage would rise up out of a pit and there would be the singer, comic or whatever, in position, facing the audience. During the rehearsal in the afternoon, everything worked fine. The stage came up with me on it, I got off and the whole platform went back down behind me. On the night of the show itself, I was dressed in a huge cape that a friend of mine had made for me from a pair of glittery curtains which were covered around the edges with feathers.

Through the speakers, I could hear, 'Ladies and gentlemen, Miss Foo Foo Lammar,' and up comes the stage with me on it. The band broke into the rehearsed 'All of Me', only this time the stage decided it would take my cape with it on its return journey. The bloody thing pulled me right over on my back, my wig fell off and the band and the audience did the only thing they could do; they all burst out laughing. The audience thought it was part of the act. Although technically it was an accident (albeit a funny one) I have to report I suffered no injuries.

However, I have unfortunately also had some bad accidents, the worst probably being the bump in the Rolls in Manchester city centre. Occasionally, I've caused accidents as well, one being at my brother Tommy's twenty-first birthday party at The Bradford Hotel on Mill Street in Manchester. One of the guests was my sister-in-law's brother-in-law (pay attention or you'll get lost), a man called Joe, who, like most of us, by the end of the night had had a few drinks too many. He said something to my sister-in-law Shirley (Tommy's wife) that offended her and she, in turn, told me. Well, anyone who knows me will tell you I can be a bit fiery at times when I've had a drink, so I went over and confronted him. We had a bit of a set-to on the pub's indoor balcony and, in the end, I lost it and threw him off it. It must have been between 15 and 20ft off the ground. When I looked over, I saw something right out of a silent slapstick movie. He'd landed on his back and was stretched out on the remains of the buffet table with trifle and sausage rolls and bits of celery all over the place.

Have you ever denied being gay?
Everyone knows I am gay and I can honestly say that I've never denied the fact. Anyway, I don't think there is anything to deny in the first place but, interestingly enough, no one, ever, whether it be a journalist, somebody from television or someone in the club, has ever come straight out and asked me, 'Are you gay?' Apart from when I'm Foo, my life is quite the opposite of being gay. I can go out with the lads, have a nice meal and a few drinks with absolutely no sexuality involved. My friends today, and you must also remember that some of these are very influential people and multi-millionaires, respect me for being Frank Pearson. In the same way that I'm not interested in what they get up to in their bedrooms, they, in turn, are not interested in what I get up to in mine.

One of the most idolised footballers in Britain today,

especially by the female fans, is Manchester United's Ryan Giggs, and he asked me if I'd attend a function early in 2002 as part of his benefit year. Incidentally, what is not common knowledge is that Ryan gave away vast sums of his money from his benefit to various charitable causes, one of which is the one closest to my heart, the Pendlebury Children's Hospital.

He asked me to attend and say a few words at the dinner as Foo Foo, which, of course, I was delighted to do. I did my few minutes, went back to my table to be followed at the mike immediately by Ryan whose opening line was, 'Well, how do I follow Foo Foo Lammar?'

When Ryan had finished his speech, he walked over to my table, thanked me for what I'd said and done and gave me a little peck on the cheek. That doesn't mean he's a homosexual. What it does mean is that he was grateful for everything I'd done for him that night and it was just his way of thanking a friend. Ryan is a down-to-earth, honest family man who knows I pose absolutely no threat to him. I think that everyone who knows me – whether it be long-standing or fleetingly, whether it be through charity work or at the club – knows that as well.

Do you diet or exercise?
I have to say that my work is both my diet and exercise. It's easy for me to go away for two weeks' holiday and easily put on a stone or more. Fortunately, when I come back home I can do three shows and it's all gone. I'm constantly on the go, always doing one thing or another, but I do know that I am also very lucky in the fact that the weight literally falls off me without me being conscious of it.

What's your favourite tipple?

For a long time it was brandy and dry ginger. Before that, it was a pint of bitter and a brandy and dry ginger when I could afford the two together. When I could, the combination made me very fiery (especially when the hecklers got too much out of hand) and earned me the nickname Battling Bella Butterworth. I'd got the nickname from another drag artist called Billy Dennis who used to tell customers in Renee Rhythm's place in Reddish, 'Don't mess with her, that's Battling Bella Butterworth.' It was a bloody awful nickname (coincidentally, it came from the places I both lived in and worked at) and I had it for quite a while but to be honest, I can't remember how I eventually lost it.

It was at this point that I decided one or the other drink would have to go and so I thought that as the bitter would undoubtedly put on more weight, that was the one. Then I found out that my blood pressure was a little on the high side and I put it down to the brandy. Whether this was true or not, I don't know, but at the time I thought, Bloody hell, this stuff's blowing my knickers off, so I stopped the brandy as well. Nowadays, I drink vodka and diet coke with ice and occasionally will have either a glass of red or white wine, with a meal but don't pretend to know anything about it.

Do you have a favourite food?

In simple terms, I like food you can eat. This *nouvelle cuisine*, or whatever it is, is no good to me. The plate's the size of a dustbin lid with a tiny spot of food in the middle. No, sorry, not for me I'm afraid. My mother used to do tripe and pig's feet and a cowheel stew so thick you could have hung wallpaper with it. By golly, though, it put hairs on your chest, something that caused me the occasional problem in later years, but I loved it. Other favourites of mine are ham shank, pea soup, potato pie and black pudding; in fact, anything, I suppose, that would be called traditional Lancashire fayre is all right by me.

Do you have a favourite restaurant?
I think restaurants today are judged on their style, their popularity, and the 'place to be' kind of thing, as opposed to the standard of food. A place I do like going to is Lounge Ten just off Cross Street near the Manchester Town Hall. I'm always well looked after when I go there and, as well as it being a very smart restaurant, the food and service are always excellent.

Were you affected by the AIDS epidemic in the 1980s?
Anybody with any sense must surely have been affected when the AIDS stories first broke. A big danger initially was the fear – even paranoia – of so-called 'normal' people assuming that it came purely from gay people. Of course, this has now been proven not to be true, but there were a lot of people initially prejudiced against gays. I'm of the opinion that there's 'filth' in both heterosexual and homosexual people; one look in the Sunday tabloids will confirm this with stories about straight men being arrested for kerb-crawling and much worse.

It still frightens and worries me now, although, I must say, not as much as it did initially, probably because more is known about it now. I have been to a few funerals in which the death has been brought on by AIDS, including a good friend of mine – a local councillor – and then a few months later I attended his partner's funeral. Both men died in horrific circumstances because, in the early days, medical science didn't have the combative drugs it has now.

The worst thing about AIDS has to be that even the cleanest-living (and looking) person can still be a carrier and not even know it themselves. I also think a lot of it is down to being responsible. I've seen girls meet boys in the club, get 'acquainted', leave the club together and I've thought to myself, I know what they're going to get up to when they get home. Sometimes they don't even wait until they get home. I've seen more than one couple at it in the alley at the side of Foo Foo's and I think, I hope they know what they're doing. As well as the gay friends I've lost through it, I've also lost a few straight ones as well. Even though, fortunately, it appears to have eased off in more recent times, people are still just as promiscuous and I don't think that will ever change.

Have you always had pets?
I love animals and, apart from my very early days, for as long as I can remember I've always had a pet. I've had a whole variety of dogs over the years including Boxers, Bichon Frises and even a German Shepherd called Zimba who died while I was out of the country on holiday. I was heartbroken when I got back home and Alan Owen and Michael Ryan told me the news. I liked the name Zimba so much when I moved to Shuttleworth some years later I called a white Alsatian after him.

To try and cheer me up after the death, Alan went out and bought me another dog. It was a massive Great Dane we christened Oscar. One memorable summer's morning (still dressed in just my underpants) I opened the front door to get the milk off the step when Oscar closed the door behind me and locked me out. In the end, I had to get rid of him because he proved too large to handle but it wasn't the last I heard of him.

I gave Oscar to Bunny Westley who ran the Burton Arms on Swan Street, and he was also one of the men who bought The Picador Club from me. It turned out that Oscar proved a handful for Bunny as well. One day, the dog decided he fancied a walk and made his way to Cantor's furniture store on the corner of Oldham Street and Ancoats Lane where he promptly decided to make himself at home on one of the beds for sale. Nobody could move Oscar and it provided such a story that the *Daily Mirror* sent a reporter and photographer along and the following day there was our former pet emblazoned across the pages of a national newspaper.

Mum, too, liked a dog around the place and, not surprisingly, used to get upset whenever one of them died. I can remember when she lost Dinky, a Pekinese, I wasn't exactly honest with her. When I found out the dog had died, I told her to leave everything to me and I'd look after the funeral. A few days went by, and I was driving around town in the Rolls with Michael when he asked me, 'Did everything go all right with the dog's funeral then?'

I was mortified. 'Bloody hell,' I said, 'I've forgotten all about it!' When Michael asked me where the dog was, I had to tell the truth. 'It's still in the boot,' I ashamedly replied. I never did tell Mum the truth. How could I tell her I'd been driving around for five days with her beloved Dinky going rigid in the back?

When I lived with Alan in Failsworth, we also had two Afghan hounds ... and an ape called Troy! I bought it from Bunny Lewis (who, for some reason, had lots of them at the time) as a birthday present for Alan. It lived in a cage in the house that was chained to a radiator in the kitchen. When I bought it, it was just a baby but, of course, as it grew older, it also grew stronger, until one day it pulled the radiator clean off the wall. We came back from Foo Foo's one night and the whole house was flooded because of this radiator damage. The bloody thing had also got out of its cage and was running around the plate rack we had high up on the wall in the lounge. The less said about the plates the better! It was going berserk in the house, throwing things all over the place, and me shouting at it at the top of my voice just seemed to annoy it even more. It was then I thought, this ape is going to have to go before it throws me out of the house! It had already done some damage to me when it had got out of its cage once before and hit me on the head with a teacup. It caused such a cut, I had to go to Ancoats Hospital for two stitches. I'm sure the ape knew I didn't like it and it caused a lot of trouble between Alan and me until I gave him the ultimatum: 'Either it goes or you go.'

Alan, on the other hand, loved the ape and used to have so much fun with it. He had a little red suit made for it, as well as a sack, and was always going along to the Post Office on Lord Lane with the ape in tow looking like a little ugly postman. Not surprisingly, they got to know him quite well at the Post Office – and very quickly!

Another night, I remember coming home around tea-time and the man from the local Co-Op was standing on my doorstep waiting for me. It seemed that Alan had put Troy on his lead and marched him down the street and into the Co-Op so he could get a bit of shopping in. Once inside the shop, the ape went mad. He leapt on to the shelves and started knocking the displays about and hurling cornflakes boxes and tins of beans at the other customers. Naturally, the manager wasn't too pleased with us and suggested in no uncertain terms that we shopped elsewhere in the future.

Alan was animal mad, but preferred a little bit more than the average dog or cat. Not long after the ape had gone, Alan came home with a horse. The fact that we had nowhere to keep it didn't stop him, so, in the end, he moved my Rolls out on to the drive and put it in the garage! Nowadays, I'm more than happy to have just the one pet, my faithful Boxer dog Sophie.

What is your shoe size?
I'm very delicate – a small eight.

What's your favourite film?
The Great Caruso starring Mario Lanza has to be my favourite. I think because I was very young when I saw it, and I could just not get over his beautiful voice. All in all, I think I must

have seen it at least 20 times. As for my favourite actor or actress, then I would definitely have to say Dame Judi Dench. I think she's a marvellous actress and I try to make sure I always find the time to watch television when she's on.

Are you scared of going to the dentist?
Not in the least because – and this is the God's honest truth – I've only ever been to the dentist once in my 65 years and that was in 1991, if I remember correctly. I was living up in Shuttleworth at the time and had a really sharp pain in my right jaw. I told one of the neighbours who, in turn, told me about a dentist she knew in nearby Ramsbottom, so I went to see him. He said I needed a filling and did it there and then and, touch wood, I've had no other trouble at all. Those teeth that have come out over the years have come out on their own. I know the pain and fear some people go through, so I can count myself very lucky when I say I've always had very good teeth. And, yes, the ones I have are all my own!

Did you watch Pop Idol *on television?*
Yes, I think I watched most of the series, actually. I thought it was good entertainment. What you must remember about the show is that the judges like Pete Waterman (whom I know very well) are not only judging and advising the singers for the singers' benefit, they are also judging for their own handbags. At the end of the day, these judges are also businessmen, so I don't blame them in the slightest. I think the two who got through to the final, Gareth and Will, both had brilliant voices and deserved to be there. What I will say

is that I think there was absolutely nothing between them; in fact, I'm sure both will go on and have terrific careers. Of course, the proof will now be in the eating and, in time, record sales will ultimately decide which one is 'the best'.

Another one of the contestants, Darius, had a real character change during the show, coming from someone who appeared really 'flash' to one who was 'ever so humble'. I'm sure someone had taken him aside and had a word with him and it obviously worked because, without it, I don't think he would have got so far. It also proved that Darius was able to take on board the constructive criticism, which was a good thing.

Have you got any tattoos?
I've got the remains of one on my left hand. I had 'Jim', after my brother, tattooed on the back of three fingers. Only the 'J' remains now and that's usually covered by the rings I wear on my wedding finger. On my left forearm, just above the wrist, I have a scar that used to read 'Tommy' after another one of my brothers. I got these done one afternoon when I was about 15 and the other two 'wagged it' from school with me. It was Tommy who actually did them himself and I don't think any of us used antiseptic at all! Tommy had 'Frank' and 'Jimmy', and Jimmy had 'Frank' and 'Tommy', so we had what you might call a matching set done. Although it seemed like a good idea at the time, I got a double battering for these tattoos.

At school, I used to sit with one hand over the other like one of Les Dawson's Lancashire housewives, while at home I'd always try to wear a long-sleeved shirt buttoned at the wrist and keep my hands in my pockets. The reasons were simple; neither the teacher at school nor anyone at home knew what we'd done and I was well aware of the consequences should they find out. I used to pinch Mum's pan-stick make-up and try to cover up the marks and, for a while, I got away with it. Of course, eventually, someone would see these tattoos and I remember the day even now.

Mum had made a bowlful of apple pie and custard and told me to take it to my gran's who lived just round the corner. It was a beautiful hot summer's day and I was wearing a short-sleeved shirt, but had not had time to apply the make-up and Mum spotted the tattoos. She was absolutely livid and stood waiting at the front door for Dad to come home with his cart at tea-time. She rushed out to see him saying, 'Have you seen the state of our Frank? He's covered in tattoos.'

Dad dropped the handles of the cart and almost before they'd hit the floor he'd leathered me with one of his shovel-like hands. Later on, he saw Jimmy's and Tommy's tattoos and, with me being the eldest and therefore the most responsible, I got another battering for my trouble. I had these tattoos for years and years, even as Foo Foo, and tried to disguise them, especially the one on my forearm, with a bracelet of some kind. In the end, I decided to have it removed and went to see a specialist in John Street who took it off with a laser. It was a lovely job and would have left no mark whatsoever if I hadn't started picking at it almost immediately after the operation.

Have you ever had a face-lift?

I haven't had a full face-lift but I have had surgery to my eyes. I used to have a scar on my forehead, right in-between the eyes, and it was thanks to a doorknob. I'd have been about 19 or so at the time, still living with my gran and was just starting out with the drag act when I did a show at the Ancoats Arms on Ancoats Lane. At that time, it was new to the majority of people and not many had actually seen it before. I think it must have been some kind of charity do, because both Gran and Mum were in the audience.

This one particular night, I'd finished the show and, as I was leaving the pub, one of the customers called me a poof. I wasn't standing for that, so I smacked him. When he got up off the floor, he ran back at at me and we both stumbled through the pub double doors. As I was getting up on my knees, the door swung back towards me and the knob struck me right between the eyes and knocked me unconscious. When I woke up, I was in Ancoats Hospital still in full make-up. What with the bruising and plaster and the make-up, I must have looked like Coco the Clown. I had four stitches in the wound and it left a mark for years. When I had the scar done years later, I also got them to tidy the eyes up a bit as well, just at the sides, nothing too drastic.

I've also had some 'tidying up' at the back of my head as well. Again, it came about because of an incident in a pub. This time it was the King's in the city centre, known locally as the Top King's because of its location at the top end of Oldham Street. I was watching the scholars walk at Whit Week, a thing I always did back then, from the doorway of the King's when a complete stranger confronted me. He turned out to be a family friend of the woman with frizzy hair that I'd set light to earlier, and had decided to take revenge for her. We had a bit of an altercation before I slapped him as well, and then just left him on the floor and walked away. Unfortunately for me, an empty pint pot was close by and he hurled it at me, striking me a beauty right on the back of the head. Once again, I was in Ancoats Hospital asking them to patch me up.

What's your favourite aftershave?
I don't wear too much aftershave personally, but when I do it's usually Polo by Ralph Lauren. Most of the time I wear Calvin Klein's Eternity for Women, both as a perfume for Foo and an aftershave for Frank, but if I was to buy any aftershave as a present it would always be Polo.

Is it all your own hair and do you dye it?
I'm very fortunate in the fact that I've still got all my own hair. I've still got a good, thick, wavy mop which I must have inherited from my father's side of the family because he was just the same even in later life. As for the dyeing part, yes, I will admit to just a drop now and again. Well, when you touch 44, you do get the odd grey hair, don't you?

Are you are a superstitious person?
I always keep to the old showbiz tradition of never whistling backstage in someone's dressing room. If you do, you have to swear, go outside, swear again and then come back in. If you

don't, the theory is you'll bring bad luck, so I try to avoid the whistling at all times. Apart from that, I'd have to say that I'm not superstitious; I believe more in reality than superstition.

I don't go to fortune-tellers or the like because I believe I'm my own fortune-teller. Everything I've done in my life, everything I've earned, I've worked hard for myself. Then, if things should go wrong, there is only me that can take the blame. I don't follow horoscopes or clairvoyants, but I will admit in believing, to a certain extent anyway, in fate. Over the years, especially as I became better known, I was asked many, many times to go into business with different people in different ventures. I turned most of them down, but on one occasion I said 'Yes' and then later on I regretted the decision and pulled out.

Metz Bar in Manchester is one example, as well as a club I sold my interest in early in 2002. After Manchester – which was a brilliant business – we opened in Liverpool and then Leeds, but, in the end, I lost over £300,000 on the project. I made the mistake of letting other people run the clubs for me and it backfired. With hindsight, it's something I should never have got involved with, purely and simply because the whole thing just went out of my control. The other clubs felt as though they didn't really belong to me and, consequently, my interest was not what it should have been. That cannot be said about Foo Foo's Palace. I've been in that place almost every day from day one and I know everything there is to know about it. Even now, as people become more aware of its impending closure, they say to me, 'You've got to open another place, but you take a back seat and let someone else run it.' I always tell them, 'No thanks, I've tried that already.' I've always tried to listen to the voice from within me. It's not let me down too much in 65 years.

What's your favourite television programme?
Despite the fact that a large number of my very good friends are in the soaps, I'm not a big fan of any of them. I just can't seem to get into them like millions of people do. Maybe it's because I can't watch them week in and week out because of various shows and functions I do, but they're just not for me. I do like the television but would have to say that I don't really have one particular favourite programme.

I do, though, like a good film – anything from musicals to horror – on television. I like adventures like *The Three Musty Queers*, old black-and-white *Tarzans* and a good old-fashioned, proper cowboy and Indian, or 'cowies' as we called them when I was younger.

Not surprisingly, I also like the Hollywood glamour movies; anything like *Gentlemen Prefer Blondes* with Jane Russell and Marilyn Monroe is guaranteed to keep me occupied from start to finish. When I see films like this, it encourages me to try and pass on that style of glamour to my customers at the club. Every time I have a new frock made, I always try and judge the reaction I'll get from the ladies the first time they see me in it. If I hear a mass 'Ooooohhhh' sound from 200 or so sharp intakes of breath, then I know I've picked a good 'un. The majority of women dream of wearing gowns and glitter and feathers, but will never get the chance to do so. Sometimes, the nearest they'll ever get is when they see me (or new movies like *Moulin Rouge*), so that's why my appearance is as important to me as it was to the beautiful and glamorous Hollywood starlets of years gone by.

Is there a television programme you'd have liked to appear in?
I would have loved to have a go at – indeed, I still would – *The Generation Game*. It's a show I've watched for years and years and have always felt that would have been my ultimate show, my forte. *The Generation Game* is perfect for Foo Foo Lammar. It's about meeting people on stage, reacting with them and then bringing the best out of them. In other words, what Foo Foo has been doing every week for the last 27 years at the Palace.

I watched my old friend Larry Grayson when he did the show in the 1970s. I loved Larry to bits and still miss him, but I believe *The Generation Game* just wasn't for him. Larry was a wonderful comic actor but was not used to working at such close quarters with the public. In time, he got more and more confident and used to it, but he looked especially out of his depth at the start and I felt for him.

I, on the other hand – and I don't want this to sound too cocky – would be perfect for it. The reason I say this is because in all my years in showbusiness, I can count on the fingers of one hand the number of times I've worked to a script. I've always said my audience is my script and I work off them and adjust my act accordingly. I come alive with a live audience; even today, I've not got an act until I step out on a stage. Many a Saturday evening I'd sit in front of the television watching the show – regardless of who the host was – acting it out as if I was actually in charge. Obviously, if I was ever given the chance to do it, the producers would have to have some control, but the actual show itself holds no fears for me at all.

I know I can adapt my performance according to whatever kind of audience I'm working to. I never use the 'F' word – I'll use 'hooking', 'ducking' and 'plucking' instead, and though it still sounds suggestive, a much wider range of people can accept it. It's also a matter of respect on my part, especially when I can play sometimes to an audience that is 90 per cent female. I'm not saying that women don't swear; indeed, a group of women together will swear a lot more than a group of men every time. I just don't think it's the done thing.

Apart from *The Generation Game*, I'd also love to do one of those celebrity *Audience With* shows. Again, primarily for the same reasons as above; in other words, I could just ad-lib my whole way through the hour-and-a-half or however long they run. Hopefully, once Foo Foo's has closed its doors for the last time, I'll have more time on my hands and will be given the chance to have a go at at least one of them.

Who would you most like to have sex with?
Bloody hell! I think it would have to be either the Muppets or the Dingles! This really is a very difficult question to answer. I spend a lot of time around celebrities, both male and female, many of whom are absolutely stunning in their looks.

Because of this I know them simply as friends and not as any sexual object, so I don't look at them in the way that strangers would. I can also appreciate a beautiful woman and will confess to admiring well-shaped women, especially those who dress well, wear nice shoes and clothes and generally look after themselves.

Do you have a favourite song?
Certainly one I'm very fond of is a song called 'My Thanks to You' which is song from a long time ago and it was one I used to sing to my mum and in concerts I did in the old folks' homes. I think it was originally released in the 1950s by a singer called Steve Conway. Whether it's a club, a pub or, indeed, a fully-fledged theatre, I cannot get off the stage – the audience simply won't let me – without singing my other two all-time favourites – 'I Am What I Am' and 'My Way'.

Do you vote?
In a word, no. The reason for this is quite simple; from the age of about 11 or 12, I worked in one job or another to try and earn a living. It's never made one iota of difference to me which party has been in power. Whether the ethics of that are right or wrong, I don't know, but that's how I feel. I'm of the opinion that no matter what colour they wear, they are all as bad as one another and no matter who says what, someone else will contradict them. I sometimes think it might be better if they just threw the whole lot of them in together. The majority of these people make a huge living and enjoy a lovely lifestyle, as, indeed, do I. However, I

know only too well how hard I've grafted to achieve mine. I've never voted once in my entire life because I believe that they are all as bad as each other and are only in the job purely for their own benefit.

Which famous person would you have liked to meet?
I would dearly have liked to have met comedian Dick Emery but, unfortunately, I never managed it. The reason for this is because I believe Dick Emery would have been a lot like me and we would have had many things in common. I don't mean in his actual act as such, but simply because Dick Emery was a man in a woman's frock. He wasn't a drag queen or anything else people might have called him; he was, like me, purely an entertainer.

Are you a religious person?
I am a Roman Catholic with the confirmation name Joseph. As to whether I'm what is called a practising one, then I suppose in the true sense of the phrase, no, I'm not. But I honestly believe that we are all practising, but we all practise in our different ways. I don't go to church every week (because of my job, sometimes, I couldn't go every week even if I wanted to), but I also believe that if you have faith and you stick to it, then that's just as good.

Are you going to Heaven or Hell?
In my humble opinion, I think (and hope!) that I will go to Heaven. I know that not everything I have done in my life has been saintly, but I can honestly say that I've done more

good in my life than bad. I don't mean the fact that I've managed to carve out a good career; I mean I think I've done more good for the general public than most average people have. Of all the bad things I've done, I'm hoping that none of them will be classed as too serious to prevent me from going through the Pearly Gates.

Have you got a police record?
I'm not sure whether you'd call it a police record as such, but I have to admit to crossing paths with 'the boys in blue' on more than one occasion; indeed, some of them are chronicled in this book. Take, for instance, the sauna bath scandal and the money fiasco in Kenya!

The times when I've been in fights and the fines that I've had have also prevented me from actually holding a licence in some clubs I've been involved with, but I've never had serious criminal convictions against my name. I've been stopped more than once for speeding and I was only reminded of one such instance recently by Allan Horrocks, the former landlord of the Halfway House in Farnworth near Bolton.

I think it must have been around 1996 or 1997, the time we were fund-raising heavily for the Pendlebury Children's Hospital. Not for the first (or last) time, I was late for the do and was belting along doing about 70mph in my pink Rolls-Royce when I was stopped by a traffic policeman. I wound the window down and listened to the officer telling me what I had done wrong. He then asked me my name.

'Star', I replied clearly, if, perhaps, a tad flamboyantly.

'First name, sir?' he asked.

'Star,' I snapped back even louder. 'Don't you know who I am?' He didn't and promptly fined me £30.

Probably my funniest 'arrest' was when I was done for importuning in the gents' toilets on Sackville Street in Manchester city centre. Looking back, it does seem very funny but, at the time, it most certainly didn't! Needless to say, it was nothing of the sort; it was just a case of being in the wrong place at the wrong time. There were three of us in drag, myself and two friends – John 'Ada' Trotter and Keith 'Kitty' White – on our way, on foot, to a do at the Rembrandt. I have to say that John was the least convincing, purely because he had a full beard and legs that wouldn't stop a pig in an alley! The other two walked on in front of me, but I was dying to use the toilet so I nipped into the gents on the opposite corner to the pub. When I got in, I lifted my frock up and answered the call. Unknown to me, the police had been watching and they followed me in the toilet and arrested me for importuning. They marched me off to Bootle Street Police Station still in full drag and I was later charged £10 – probably the most expensive piss in history!

Friends —
In Their Own
Words

I THINK IT WAS George Best who said something along the lines of, 'I'm currently writing my autobiography, so if anyone can tell me where I was between 1973 and 1978, I'd appreciate it.'

Well, I have to say that I'm not that bad at the moment, but will admit that I do need the occasional prompt. My life has certainly been a hectic one and the number of people I've encountered, either in the back streets of Ancoats, my working life in the mills or throughout my career in showbiz, must run into the thousands. I apologise here and now if I've missed anyone out and can assure them it wasn't deliberate.

Because of this, I contacted my good friends at BBC GMR (especially Fred 'Chunky Baby' Fielder) and the *Manchester*

Evening News and asked if they could let people know about my book and also to ask any listeners or readers who knew me from 'the good old days' to get in touch and let me have their recollections. I was delighted not only by the response I received, but it also gave me a chance to remember the lovely people I've lost touch with over the years. Please accept my apologies for this and I'd like to thank each and every one of you for all the good wishes I received, along with some lovely stories.

Here are just a few of the many I received.

Audrey Gordon
(Former work colleague at Butterworth's)
I first remember Frank (or Foo Foo) when I was about 18 years old on a bus going into town from Clayton. The bus pulled up at the stop on Grey Mare Lane and Frank staggered upstairs in his stilettos and tight mini-skirt. As he passed me and my friends, he said, 'Hello, girls; I like your handbags!'

I met Foo Foo many times after that, especially when she used to sing around the Bradford area of Manchester in the early 1960s. One particular place was the Prince of Wales on the corner of Forge Lane where she was also the compére. Every night we were guaranteed a great time, especially when she used to get volunteers up on stage and, remember, these were the days when you could understand the words as well!

Frank also played the Bradford Labour Club and, in those days, seeing someone in drag wasn't as commonplace as it is today. I remember seeing him one night and he really struggled with a dodgy microphone. Well, I wasn't having any of that so I started clapping my hands and shouting my head off to try and encourage him. By the time he'd finished, the club appreciated both our efforts and they realised just what a really good 'turn' he was. Frank showed his appreciation later when he came over to my table and chatted with both myself and my husband Brian.

Frank later became a manager at Butterworth's paper factory on Pollard Street where he was very popular with everyone. I remember Frank would be singing all the time. I used to go around singing a lot as well; my particular favourite was 'The Yellow Rose of Texas'. One day, my sister and I were sat around a hole on the sixth floor sorting out paper which we then dropped through to the ground floor. Frank came up to us and shouted, 'Eh, come on you Andrews' Sisters. Why aren't you singing?' I don't think he appreciated the fact that we were balanced about 100ft up and needed to concentrate to keep our balance!

I've seen Foo Foo lots of times over the years and am delighted to see she has 'gone up in the world' and been so successful. When I hear the younger ones today talk about the nights they've enjoyed at her club in town, I envy them because I'd love to have seen a hen party in full flow.

Frank came up to my local club, The Fitzroy in Droylsden, a few years ago and it was a really great night. I got in very early so as to get a front row seat. Alas, Foo Foo didn't recognise either my husband or me (time does that, you know!) but I would have thought he'd have at least remembered my bright red hair!

I hope Frank has great success with the book and with everything else he does in the future. For such an outgoing and talented man, he is still very friendly to everyone and I also know just how devoted he was to his late mother.

Good luck and best wishes.

Liz Dawn

(Fellow charity worker and Coronation Street*'s Vera Duckworth)*

I've always thought Frank should have been recognised for all the good work he's done over the years. I think he should get an MBE or even a statue right in the middle of Albert Square! Whatever it is, Manchester, at least, should publicly recognise him for his efforts. He's done so much for Manchester charities over the years, if people asked me for a list, I wouldn't know where to start. And I don't just mean the well-known ones either. There are literally hundreds of individuals he's helped throughout his career who largely go unnoticed.

I can honestly say I've never known anyone else quite like him, and I consider myself very lucky to be able to say we've worked together so many times (and had so much fun) I've lost count. Even though we've not spoken as much in the last couple of years or so, what with one thing or another, I know that if I really needed Frank's help for anything, he'd always be there for me. Likewise, he knows the same about me. I say a prayer for him every day in the hope that he beats the cancer once and for all.

I'm sure he remembers the story about me not knowing who the famous artist Harold Riley was when we were both guests at a party Frank held in Shuttleworth. I wonder if he remembers Harold standing up later and addressing the whole room with 'I believe someone here thinks I'm a painter and decorator!' I loved that house and spent many happy hours there.

I've known Frank for about 30 years and you couldn't wish to meet a nicer, more genuine man; one I'm delighted to call a great friend.

Rusty King

(Nightclub compère and long-standing friend)

I'm 62 now and have known Frank since I was 14, so you could say we go back a long way. I've lost count not only of the number of times we've worked together in pubs and clubs in and around Manchester, but also of the number of times Frank has borrowed my sister's clothes for a show – and never returned them! As well as working together, we also socialised a lot, especially on a Friday or Saturday night.

I can't remember the exact reason, but one Friday night (around 1958, I think) we thought we'd have a change from Manchester and decided to go to Liverpool. We missed the last train coming back and had to spend the night on the floor of a house belonging to two lads we'd met in a bar.

When we woke up we thought we'd make a day of it and set out for a bit of shopping. We were in a department store when Frank stole a pair of eyelashes. As it was the first pair he'd ever tried, he wanted to find the nearest toilets as quickly as possible so he could have a look at them. When he put them in, he turned round to me and said, 'These feel awful.'

I replied, 'I'm not surprised, you've got them in upside down!'

Frank said, 'Thank God for that, I thought I was in jail!'

Frank seemed to like this store so much that I can remember him taking me to the Manchester branch some time later for some Christmas shopping. It was a bitterly cold day, blowing a blizzard, and I was well wrapped up in my thick woollen duffle coat. We spent about 20 minutes in the store when Frank decides he'd had enough and says, 'Come on, there's nothing in here,' and so we left.

When I got outside, I put my hood up to combat the snow, only to find myself covered in bottles of perfume and an assortment of brooches. Frank had been using the hood of my coat for shoplifting! It was then that I realised why he'd been patting me on the shoulder so much! I set off running up the street (or should I say slipping and sliding because of the ice underfoot) with bottles and jewellery falling out all over the place.

In the late 1950s and early 1960s, neither of us had much money (in fact, we were bloody skint, more often than not), but Frank always liked to look his best and made sure he was as well groomed as possible. The same can be said of him today. I can remember one particular Friday night he came round to my house with his usual, 'What are you up to, then?'

I said I wanted to go out but had no money and also had nothing to wear. I told Frank I'd seen a beautiful suit in Sid Vernon's tailor's shop on Ashton New Road for £3, but I could only raise £1. Frank said not to worry and the next day he came back with the £2 and off we went to buy the suit. I know Frank didn't have any money at the time and don't know where he got it from. Mind you, I didn't ask him and he didn't bother to tell me, either!

He has always been good with money. Often, we'd go out for an evening with two shillings, be in the pub drinking until kicking-out time, and return home with two and six in our pockets. To this day, I don't know how he managed it.

I'll let you into a little secret about his beautiful, wavy hair. When I'd go round to his gran's before we went to the pub, more often than not, Frank was on his knees in front of the coal fire – with brown paper in one hand and a red-hot poker in the other. The crafty bugger was putting his rollers in! I can still hear his mum mumbling, 'Just look what he's doing to himself.'

Even now, we still see each other every other week when Frank tries to come round to my house for a meal. Like I say, I've known him a long time and I know what to feed him. Tater 'ash is always good, none of this modern stuff for Frank. It's got to be good old British cooking every time. I remember having a meal with him once in a restaurant and he ordered scallops. When they were delivered, Frank cut one open and, to his horror, he found fish inside. He said, 'I can't eat this muck.' He was expecting a more familiar (at least to him) potato one!

I look forward to these meals together and long may they continue.

All the best, mate.

Brian Ingham

(Friend of member of staff at Frank's sauna)

Many years ago, Frank had a sauna in Manchester close to the cathedral and a mate of mine, Bill Gibson, used to work there for him. One day, I went to the sauna to wait for Bill to finish work and we were going to go home together. Just as we were ready to leave, Frank came rushing in waving a copy of the *Manchester Evening News* in the air shouting, 'I'll sue the lot of them,' in his best Foo Foo voice, of course.

Everyone in the place came rushing round and we said, 'What is it, Frank?' We couldn't stop laughing when he told us. It seems that the ad he'd placed in that night's paper billed him as 'Miss Poo Poo Lammar'! Fortunately, he calmed down in the end and never did sue the paper.

Bill Tarmey

(Bradford schoolboy who later became Coronation Street's *Jack Duckworth)*

I was born and brought up on the same terraced street, Butterworth Street, in Bradford, Manchester. Admittedly, I'm considerably younger(!) than Frank, but when you look at how we both started out, neither of us have done too badly.

If it was possible to chronicle every single piece of charity work Frank has done over the years, people would be absolutely amazed. In an age when so-called celebrities will turn up – and only turn up – when the press and fanfares are there, it's so refreshing to have someone like Frank who'll turn up anywhere, any time and do the business just for the charity. He just does everything quietly, with no fuss or frills, and whether the press are there or not makes no difference.

I agree wholeheartedly with Liz Dawn (just like I always do on the *Street*) when she says it's such a shame that Frank's not been recognised officially for all the charity work he's done. I love him to bits and, for my money, he deserves the biggest 'gong' going.

Jean Thornton

(Former work colleague at Butterworth's)

Although I only worked at Butterworth's for about six months before leaving to have a baby, I still have fond memories of Frank. Along with my sister Marion (Corrigan), I was employed as a baler and we worked alongside Leah Massey, and two other ladies called Edna and Lizzie Anne. Frank had nicknames for most of the girls and I remember one in particular whom everyone knew as 'old Mary' (I remember she always arrived late for work, as well), but Frank christened her 'Greasy Ankles'.

He was a lovely man to work for, always singing and very quick-witted. He was also very clever and I've lost count of the times he managed to wheedle out of things even during the short time I knew him. I saw him many times singing in various pubs in the evenings after work and remember one occasion when he was on stage and I walked through the pub doors. He saw me coming in and announced to everyone, 'Here she comes; the only woman I know who can stick a banana up her nose sideways!' He was a wonderful singer and I always knew he'd go on to great things, and so it's proved.

One final recollection concerned a night out the girls had. We were all walking down the street to the pub apart from

Lizzie Anne who was frantically struggling to keep up but had fallen a few paces behind. Frank spotted this and said, 'Just look at her; she's got a face like a Belisha beacon.' He then went back to the front of the group and continued hoola-hooping his way down the middle of the road! I don't think he ever knew the meaning of the word shame!

Roy 'Chubby' Brown
(A man who needs no introduction – so he's not getting one!)
Yes, poor Frank. What can I say about him? To me, he will always be therapubic. The trouble is, his passport photograph does him an injustice; it's the fucking spittin' image of him!

I first met him when he was thinking of changing his name by deed poll to Puff Pastry. I fell in love with his personality within a second. Shaking hands would have sufficed but the tongue down the throat was a bit much! He's given showbusiness the best two years of his life. One of them was just after the war and the other one was in the Sixties. And yet he's such a professional. If you exposed yourself to him, he'd probably do ten minutes of funnies about your dick.

If I can be serious though for a minute, I tell people all the time, 'If you ever need cheering up, go and see Foo Foo Lammar. He's a star in every way.'

Winnie Fitzpatrick
(Friend and occasional singing partner)
I've known Frank for almost 50 years, from the days when I was the teenager Winnie Trainor and he used to sing in the Robin Hood near Piccadilly Station. I did a bit of singing

myself at the time in the pubs in Hulme where I used to live, and when I had a night out in town with my sister, we'd always go and see Frank. Although I was confident singing to my friends near home, singing in town was another matter, but even though I was a bit nervous, Frank never failed to get me up on stage and join in with him. I remember Frank used to sing regularly alongside the piano with another fellow by the name of Tony (Antoinette) Lloyd, who had bleached-blonde hair and the pair of them were well known for the song 'Sisters'.

I also knew his mum quite well, initially from when she worked in the hairdresser's I used to go to in Hulme, and later when I ran a bar in Tenerife. Frank would take his mum and a friend out most years around Easter time and they'd always make a point of looking us up and we had some great times together talking about the good old days.

Not too far from where I'm living at the moment is the Wythenshawe Forum and Frank made sure all my family had free tickets for when he played *The Rocky Horror Show* there a few years back.

I've been to Foo Foo's Palace many times and never failed to really enjoy myself. Frank is a lovely person and someone who'll never change or forget his friends, and I wish him all the best in the future.

One final thing – back in the 1950s, I had a lovely two-piece dress suit with a long skirt and pom-poms on the jacket. I loved this outfit nearly as much as Frank did. Looking back, I'm sure he wore it more than I did! He certainly borrowed it enough times.

Maxine Barrie

(The best Shirley Bassey impersonator in the business).

I first met Frank what seems like 100 years ago now, as I've known him for so long. Our paths crossed many times in the various pubs and clubs we played, but we were really only on what you might call nodding terms. The first time we had any sort of a real conversation was at an Equity meeting, held in those days at the Rembrandt on Monday evenings.

Frank came in around 9.00pm, dressed in the full drag complete with feathers and we began to chat. I don't know if he'd been working or was on his way to work; I never thought to ask, to be honest! He told me he was interested in buying a club and asked me for my opinion. The club in question was The Celebrity Club on Dale Street and I told him that I knew it even before then as La Petite, going on to say, 'I think you should and take a chance.' Fortunately, he did and, of course, later on Foo Foo's Palace was born.

When Frank got the new club up and running, he gave me the chance to perform there many, many times and would always look after me. He's given me countless dresses over the years (the ones he thought were not over the top enough for him but were perfect for me) and lots of feather boas and jewellery.

On one occasion, I was getting ready to go out on stage at Foo Foo's when I realised I'd forgotten my shoes. 'Don't worry, you can borrow a pair of mine,' said Frank, and promptly produced a beautiful pair of sparkling high-heels. They were perfect apart from one thing; unfortunately, they were two sizes too big. I normally take a six whereas Frank takes an eight. I had no option but to do my whole act clomping around the stage hoping no one would notice! Happily for me, I don't think anyone did.

Nowadays, we travel down to London regularly on the train and then via taxi to Berwick Street in Soho, which is *the* street for dress material and stagewear anywhere. We can easily spend hours in the stores (as well as a small fortune – the material is to die for; upwards of £100 per metre) before a quick cup of tea and then back on the train again. The first time I took Frank into one particular shop, he screamed out in amazement and then spent £1,800 in an hour. Once we've decided on the material, we both have our dresses made by the same dressmaker in Barnsley.

As Frank has been bold enough finally to reveal his true age, I'll now reveal mine – I'm 29 plus VAT! Here's to the next 100 years of true friendship.

Alf Solomon
(Long-standing friend and holiday-maker)
Frank and I go back a long, long way; in fact, I used to live in the next street to his gran's so I've known him for the best part of 50 years or so. I've got many happy memories of him over that period (including the time I decorated his bungalow in Failsworth), but arguably the best times we ever had together were the times we went away on holiday.

It would have been the back end of the 1960s and the early 1970s when a group of us used to go to Spain, with Benidorm and Sitges becoming our favourite destinations. I can remember arranging the bookings for everyone one year when we travelled with the aptly named Gaytours. We were met by coach from their offices on Deansgate and taken to Manchester Airport ready for the flight to Benidorm. We had 15 days' full board at the Hotel Torredorade for 59 guineas (the best part of £64) and that included the flight! Frank impressed the management at another hotel in Sitges once so much that they wouldn't let him out in the evenings and he became their regular cabaret for the whole two-week stay.

It should come as no surprise to anyone that he was just as outrageous all those years ago. Once we were on the beach in Sitges and Frank was fascinated by a poor woman who was really struggling to get rid of all these bits of jewellery and trinkets she was trying to sell. In the end, Frank had enough and said, 'Watch this.' He walked over to the woman, somehow managed to persuade her to lend him her dress, shoes and bag, and the next thing we knew he was off down the beach. Less than ten minutes later, he was back with an empty bag and a handful of pesetas. It was a remarkable sight and, fortunately, I was on hand with my camera to record it for all time.

Bernard Manning
(Another good friend who needs no introduction)
Without doubt, Frank Lammar is one of the finest drag artists in the country and a man who has raised millions of pounds for charity. I've done loads of shows with him over the years for all kinds of denominations and colours, and I know just how much hard work he puts in.

He's wonderful company to be with, is very funny and

everyone – certainly in the north of England – who knows him thinks the world of him. Because of his involvement in nightclubs all these years, I also know just how much work he's also been able to give to other artists and musicians. In fact, the only problem I have with him is that he's a Manchester United supporter!

It's a funny business this showbusiness, and you can fall ill at any time, but the show must go on. I wish him continued success in his unsuccessful career!

Terry Maffia
(Former work colleague at Butterworth's)
I met Frank for the first time in 1969 at what was a difficult time in my life. I'd been (harshly) made redundant and my wife was expecting our first baby when I applied for a job I'd seen advertised in the office at Butterworth's. I had the interview and, fortunately, they offered me the job, but I must admit to having some regrets on my first morning there.

I like to have a laugh myself, but felt I'd possibly made a mistake with the job because everyone else there seemed very dour and serious. Midway through the morning, Frank breezed into the office. He was very smartly dressed (as he always was) and I remember him wearing a brown suit with a thick mop of wavy hair on top. In fact, looking back, I seem to remember he was always predominantly dressed in brown the whole time I knew him. When he spoke, he had what you might call a camp voice. I'd never seen or heard anything like this before, and it brightened the day up for me from then on.

Almost from the outset, I got on very well with him. I think one reason is that we've got a similar sense of humour. I never saw him as being what today is termed 'gay'; in fact, the word meant something very different back then. I just saw him as camp and very funny. I also saw him as a bit of a revelation. He was not only friendly to everyone who worked there, but compassionate as well. Although he held a senior management position, he treated everybody in the same, fair way and I class him as certainly the first equal opportunity employer I'd ever come across.

The working conditions were not the greatest I'd ever seen, and the poor girls who worked in the sheds had to put up with rats and who knows what else. Without being too critical or insulting, I'm sure some of these girls were dysfunctional, and yet Frank spent as much time talking to the most junior workers as he did to the directors. Class or background made no difference at all to Frank; to him, everybody deserved the same treatment and decency.

There was a flight of steps leading from the office into the courtyard at Butterworth's, and at the end of this yard was an area where the drivers used to park the wagons. Many times I've seen the drivers, and these were huge, burly men, huddled together having a smoke before taking the wagons out in the morning. Frank would then come strutting down the yard – as usual, immaculately dressed – and shout at the top of his voice, 'Come on, you load of fisherwomen. Get these lorries out.' To a man, every single one of them immediately stopped talking and got on to the lorries. I never saw one answer him back, such was the respect he was held in. I don't think any other member of the management team would have got the same response.

During my time at Butterworth's, I never felt what you might call 'stretched'. Indeed, most people I knew there seemed to have completed their week's work by Wednesday. To fill in the spare time, we created a pushpenny league and knockout cup which everyone, from the directors downwards, played in. People became quite skilled and it got quite serious as time went on with everyone working out the best ways of knocking the old sixpence through the opponents' goal with an old penny. My own personal favourite was the edge of a cigarette box, but one director's son – Dave Tarbuck, who also worked there – used a silver steel comb that was a very popular fashion accessory at the time.

I got through to the final once and played against Dave Tarbuck. I was beating him quite easily but, unfortunately for me, I scored one goal too many and it upset him. He lost control and threw the steel comb at me and it hit me just above the eyebrow.

Frank had been watching the game along with a few others and lost his temper, a thing I'd never seen him do at all before. He leapt at Tarbuck (whom we all used to think was bit 'nerdy') grabbed him by the tie and picked up a pair of scissors from a nearby desk. He was just about to cut his tie off when Tarbuck senior entered the room and asked what was going on. Frank told him what had happened and the two Tarbucks left the room and made their way to the board room next-door. The son got a terrible dressing down from his father, so loud, in fact, that we all heard every single word as the conversation came through the walls.

Nothing was ever said to Frank about the whole episode, and I still remember that incident as just one example of the way he treated and stood up for his workforce.

After Butterworth's, I got a sales job with Smith Corona typewriters. I'd been there for quite a while when one day, I got a phonecall from my manager saying that our Midlands sales rep and her husband were coming up to Manchester on business and would my wife and I mind taking them out for a meal and to a club in the evening?

We had a nice meal at a restaurant in town and then ended up in The Picador Club which, in all honesty, I'd never heard of up until then. We found some nice seats close to the stage when I heard, 'Cooee, lovey!' from the drag act on stage. Well, like most people, I turned round to see who he was shouting to. I then heard, 'Don't turn your back on me, you bitch! I remember when we used to kiss over our sandwiches.'

Unbeknown to me it was Frank as large as life and as bold as ever. Everybody turned to look at me and I've never been so embarrassed in my entire life. My wife and the couple from the Midlands put two and two together and must have come up with something awful!

Bryan Robson
(Former Manchester United and England captain)
I got to know Frank when we worked together on the scanner appeal and, for me, he's absolutely brilliant. I went to his club a few times when he did shows there for the appeal and he was always hilarious. Not only is he very funny, he's also a really good singer as well.

What impresses me most, though, about Frank is the sheer amount of work he does for charity. I think he deserves everything – and more – he's achieved in showbusiness purely on that alone.

Frank Burn

(Disc Jockey and undertaker – honestly!)

I was 'Frank the DJ' at the Royal George pub on Lever Street and every year I'd DJ at Frank's mum's birthday party. I'd known both Frank and his mum for a good few years prior to me working at the Royal George. In fact, I'd first met them when they were regulars at another pub I worked in, the Hat and Feathers on Mason Street. The landlady of the Hat and Feathers, Carol Gorman, was a really good friend of Leah's and I've known many an occasion when the pub closed and Frank's mum would stay behind for another drink.

I remember one particular year when Frank arranged his mum's party at the Royal George. I managed to persuade Pete and Ronnie from Sweet Charity and Frank to get up on stage and mime their way through a Sixties melody as the fictitious band Foo Foo and the Chariots. It was very funny and everyone loved it. From as long as I've known him, Frank has always had a soft spot for music from the Fifties and Sixties.

In 1981, I think it was, I organised a show with Emile Ford (of The Checkmates fame) at the Royal British Legion Club on Regent Road in Salford. Somehow, we packed in 500 people in a place that should have held just half that. After that, I thought I'd do *The Frank Lammar Show* and charged £2.50 a head. Unfortunately, people at that time weren't used to paying that much (it was normally around the 50p mark) and the turnout was very poor. In the end, the most I could raise was £70 and handed it over to Frank, telling him what I thought was the reason for the disappointing turnout. He said, 'I thought you were charging a bit much for me. But never mind, this £70 will come in handy. It'll just pay for my car tax!'

I've had a lot of fun with Frank over the years, but was also involved in probably the worst time of his life as well – his mum's funeral. In my daytime job as undertaker with Michael Kennedy's, I drove the hearse that day. It was a very big funeral with two hearses, actually – one purely for the flowers – and eight limousines. Frank was, not surprisingly, devastated, but went on to do his show as planned (I know because I saw it) that same Friday evening. I thought it was a remarkable thing to do, and I can still see and hear the standing ovation he got that night.

When my son David was born 14 years ago, I asked Frank if he'd like to be the godfather. I was delighted when he agreed, and he carried out his duties at the christening at St Luke's Church on Kenyon Lane in his usual professional style. Afterwards, of course, we changed his title to that of godmother, but it never bothered him in the slightest and he took it all in good fun. In fact, he still does today.

Yvonne Joseph and Geremy Phillips
(Secretary and Chairman, Manchester and District Variety Branch, Equity)
We have known Frank Foo Foo Lammar since his early days in the business when he worked at the Bakers' Union Club in Moss Side. Frank worked very hard to make his act strong and

professional and soon fronted his own club, The Picador, which became very popular with both the public and theatrical people who enjoyed the relaxed atmosphere of the venue. He has since enjoyed some 27 years at Foo Foo's Palace, proving that he could stay abreast of the times and maintain popularity with the public.

Perhaps less well known is his generosity to fellow artistes, particularly to those who have fallen on hard times. As chairman and secretary of the Manchester and District Variety Branch of Equity, we are delighted to know Frank and to acknowledge his durability and success. We are also grateful for all the laughter and happy memories we have shared with him over the years.

Susie Mathis
(Broadcaster and fellow charity worker)
The first time I ever came across Frank was way back in 1967 at Mr Smith's when I was singing with The Dolly Set, a few years before the days of The Paper Dolls.

The nightclub scene in Manchester back then was absolutely bursting at the seams. When I say there were something like 50 cabaret shows on at any one time, it's no exaggeration. Like Frank, we, too, were trying to make it big at the time and, because of this, I've always had an incredible empathy with him. There was something about him even then and people seemed to flock to Frank almost instantly. I've said many times that I wished I'd have found a heterosexual guy I felt the same about. I'm absolutely certain that, had Frank not been gay, we would undoubtedly have married. There's always been a very special bond between us. We've always been able to tell each other about our bad times and crumbling relationships. We are as close to each other as it is possible for a couple to be without having sex and, honestly, despite what others might say and think, we've *never* had sex.

In those early days, Frank and I would go to The Piccadilly Club regularly where people like Tommy Cooper and the Manchester comedian Gerry Harris would also go for a drink. We've always got pissed together brilliantly, and that includes the times when I've needed his shoulder to cry on as well!

As time has gone on and we've done all the charity work together, day after day, night after night, we've become almost like a double act, with me constantly being the stooge. We've done many auctions together for various good causes, as well as for celebrities such as Ian Botham and Bill Podmore from *Coronation Street*, with me constantly trying (and failing) to ask Frank not to swear. Of course, I never manage it, but the wonderful way Frank abuses the audience, embarrasses people or even compels them into giving is a sight to behold.

Whatever you try to do, you just know that Frank will top it. I can remember clearly (and I've got a photograph to prove this) sitting in Foo Foo's Palace with a fully-grown live duck sitting on my lap. Although I don't look drunk in the photograph, I can't remember at all why I've got a duck with me! Not even I could have taken it in with me, and heaven knows why one should have been in the club in the first place.

Even though Frank has arguably made his name as the legendary Foo Foo, every time I see him like that (and I've seen him countless times over the years) I can't wait for him to get out of the frock. Personally (even though I adore him, anyway) I much prefer Frank in the dinner suit and bow-tie singing 'My Way'.

We've both got outrageous streaks within us and we always manage to bring out the best and the worst in each other. Whatever family events (such as weddings, birthdays and celebrations) on either side have taken place over the last 30-odd years, the other one has always been there. Every single one of these unquestionably ends with us both sobbing our hearts out because we're just the same emotionally. Another feature of the end of any party we both attend is that he will never let me go home!

When Frank turned 50, all his friends arranged a big celebratory party for him at the Portland Hotel, a very posh do with ballgowns and dinner suits the order of the day. I was on air at 9.00am the following morning and, despite my pleas for a least a few hours' sleep, Frank, as usual, would just not let me go home. In the end, I finally managed to leave the hotel at 8.40am and walked across the road to Piccadilly Radio still in full evening wear and did the whole show in the same clothes. The highlight for him was then going back to his bedroom, turning the radio on and listening (and, no doubt, laughing) at just how bad I sounded!

People always see the outgoing side of Frank. They never see him during the dark times, such as when his mum died and when he had plastic surgery around the eyes. I, on the other hand, have seen him during some very dark times so I know full well just how deep his feelings can go. And yet, he never seems to complain and always tries his hardest to gloss over things, almost dismissing them without a second glance.

Along with Bryan Robson, I went to see him in hospital after he'd had the plastic surgery and he looked terrible. He looked like the Elephant Man! Bryan didn't know exactly why Frank was in, and we were both terribly shocked when we saw him. As well as the obvious swelling and bruises caused by the operation, he'd also had a bad time with the anaesthetic and was very depressed.

Despite this, we still found time for a little light relief. On the television in Frank's room was the classic horror movie *Frankenstein*. I looked at Frank, then at the television, and back to Frank again, before saying, 'Do you know, I can't tell the difference!' Even when he came out of the hospital and returned home, it was still quite a while before the depression lifted and he was back to his usual self. I'm sure he was still missing his mum at this time as well and, unusually, things got on top of him. In all the years I've known him, I can honestly say that was the lowest I've ever seen him.

Frank has always been there for me at the most important, difficult and troublesome times of my life, and I don't think I'll ever be able to repay him properly. He's a lovely, lovely man and I love him to bits.

10

All Change at the Palace

*A*T THE TIME OF writing, it is my intention to close the doors at Foo Foo's Palace for the very last time on 26 December 2002. Mind you, I'd planned to close it last year and we're still going strong! I have to say that the closure is not through any choice of mine. I've always said that as long as I've got an ounce of energy left in my body, I'll keep the place open. It's simply the fact that the lease on the property is up and the whole area is due for development. I don't think anything concrete has been decided yet about the future of the building itself, although I have heard a few whispers that suggested what was once the stage at Foo Foo's Palace will become the living room of some upmarket flat.

Going back some eight years or so, I was very close to having the club closed for me then because of the state of the floor. There was talk of us moving to new premises across Dale Street while £250,000 worth of repairs were carried out but, in the end, we managed to patch things up (with some well-placed wig blocks!) sufficiently to pass the next building examination. That wouldn't be the case today, though, I'm sure. Even if the lease wasn't up shortly, there's no way it would be allowed to remain open as a nightclub simply because of the floor and the new building safety legislation. It's a little-known fact that although the club itself is below street level, there's another couple of levels (various cellars and what have you) below that.

Michael Ryan is my manager at Foo Foo's Palace and has been in the position for something like 20 years. He'd been with me at The Picador as both a barman and general odd-job man, and came with me to Dale Street not long after I bought The Celebrity Club. Michael then started courting my niece Debbie and they eventually married and, nowadays, as well as his commitments to me and Foo Foo's Palace, he also looks after Monroe's. I'll let Michael continue the story.

I first met Frank in 1975. Back then, I was bored to tears working for Manchester City Council and was asked by John Foster, at the time manager of The Picador, if I'd be interested in some part-time bar work. I said 'Yes', but, to be honest, I had no experience of it at all then; in fact, I didn't even know what a gin and tonic was!

Working at The Picador was a real experience. The customers didn't throw bottles at you; they threw the barrels!

It was so hazardous for the DJ Tommy, that he played his records from inside a cage.

I stayed on for a short time after Frank had bought Foo Foo's and then they asked me if I'd help them out just for one Saturday at the new place. So, again, I said 'Yes', and this one Saturday night led to me doing the office work, and eventually turned into a full-time job. Over the years, I've worked for Frank in probably every club he's ever been involved with – from the sauna to the Metz – in one capacity or another. For a while, I was box-office manager at Foo Foo's and, finally, nowadays I'm his personal manager.

We've been through some very interesting times together, some of which neither of us would wish to see in print! Among my many duties as his manager are booking and arranging his outside appearances, making sure all the bills are paid on time and generally just being there if he needs anything.

Frank is a real trouper and hates missing a performance. Even when he had trouble with the gout and, more recently, with the cancer, he's always been determined, in true showbiz style, that 'the show must go on'. I can remember some time in the early 1980s, I think it was, he was so ill with 'flu everyone thought he had pneumonia. He was laid out in the dressing room prior to the show covered in a blanket with the fire full on looking terrible, so bad, in fact, I insisted on calling the doctor. When the doctor saw him, he immediately said Frank shouldn't work and prescribed some tablets for him. As soon as the doctor had left, Frank took two tablets, managed somehow to get to his feet and promptly went out and did a three-hour show. Not one person in the audience was any the wiser. Mind you, he was absolutely knackered afterwards!

Frank's opinion of hard work and never taking time off doesn't stop with himself. I had a minor operation a few years back in the BUPA Hospital in Whalley Range and was just coming through the anaesthetic when he telephoned. Even though I still wasn't fully awake, I thought at the time, isn't that nice, him checking to see how I am. Nothing was further from the truth. The first thing he said to me was, 'Where's the VAT book?'

Although he's done all the charity work for hospitals over the years, he'll tell you himself he personally doesn't like making hospital visits and has to be strong-armed into going to see anyone. When he did finally come to see me, almost before he'd got into the room, he said, 'When are you coming back?'

On the outside, Frank appears to be a sort of hard businessman-type and yet, having worked for him for so long, I know what he's really like. What people see is not necessarily what you get with Frank. Underneath the complex character and the bravado, if you like, he's really very soft. Sometimes he's too soft for his own good. There are so many people in Manchester who wouldn't be where they are today without his help over the years.

Not too long ago, he helped out an old friend who wanted to buy a bar in Lanzarote. I have to say that that particular loan was paid back fully, but there have been many occasions when he's lent money (and always quietly) and not got a penny of it back. There are quite a few people currently in business who've forgotten how it all started for them and, remember, I should know; it's me that keeps all his books!

Frank has undoubtedly lived for his work. Probably because he has no children of his own, he has poured himself into his work, although, having said that, he dotes terribly on all his brothers' children. Some people might think this is strange, but I think he would have made a really good father.

The night before Frank went into hospital for his kidney operation last year was a really tearful show for the staff. As far as the punters were concerned, it was just another show for him, but the staff knew all too well, it could possibly be the last time we'd ever see him on stage. There were 20-odd of us trying to hold back the tears and I'm not ashamed to admit it, I don't think any of us quite managed for the whole show. We tried as best we could to keep the place going while he convalesced, but although the shows themselves were still good – and I can't remember one customer complaining – Foo Foo's without Foo Foo is just not the same.

Frank once said to me, 'We've argued for the last 20-odd years.' We've certainly had a few disagreements during that time, but we've always been able to work things out and bounce ideas off each other, which I think at times both of us needed.

* * *

It will be a very sad day when the lease expires and we finally close the doors at Foo Foo's. To this day, 27 years after I bought the place, despite sickness, building alterations and slightly suspect flooring, those doors have always been open. Without getting too morbid and sentimental (although I see no real reason as to why I shouldn't be after all the years I've put into it), when that final day comes, Manchester will have lost one of its most famous landmarks and certainly a bastion of the nightclub scene. With Bernard Manning only making a very rare appearance nowadays at his 'world famous Embassy Club', Foo Foo's Palace is really the last of Manchester's great cabaret venues.

In the early part of the year, the club is open only on Friday and Saturday nights and has a capacity of 450 people. As the nights draw in and Christmas approaches, this changes to five nights a week with every night filled to capacity.

Although the club will no longer be with us, Foo Foo herself will still be around. I plan to do some shows around the country and, who knows, I might even spend a good few months at a time at my place in Marbella before coming back to England to 'tread the boards' again. Neither have I ruled out entirely the possibility of occasionally doing a smaller version of the same basic show I do now, but that will depend on various things, not least of all my health.

If losing the club will be a big wrench for me, it will be exactly the same for the staff as well – including the band, they number somewhere in the region of 40 people – some of whom have been with me for the proverbial donkey's years. I suppose if there is any consolation, then it's the fact that 90 per cent of them are over retirement age anyway, and they've known the club was closing for the last 18 months or so, so at least it won't be too much of a shock. The only reason they are still working today is because they have been as loyal to me as I have to them.

With barmaids of 68 (Jean Carroll) and 79 (Irene Marfleet), I think it's probably about time I gave them a break anyway!

My Polish chef (John Davies – a good, old-fashioned Polish name!) is also 79 and came to me after working at The Waldorf Hotel in London and later at The Old Shambles pub near the cathedral. Being semi-retired, he came looking for a part-time job about 20 years ago. Good job he wasn't looking for something permanent!

Jimmy Brady, my 28st DJ, originally began working for me as a bouncer on the door. As you can imagine, he's quite a big lad! I had another DJ who one night up and left to go to Blackpool, so I had no option but to throw Jimmy into the box. That was 22 years ago and he's still in it.

The down side of all this, though, is that for most of them it's not work; it's purely the way they socialise and it also gets them out of the house more than they would do otherwise. I don't consider them as my workforce; I consider them as my family. I know full well that without the efforts and loyalty of the staff at the club, I would not have achieved half as much as I have done. Even staff who no longer work at the club (mainly due to their retirement) still call in occasionally to see old friends and have a night out, which keeps the family going.

The musicians who currently work at the club are not employed exclusively by Foo Foo's. They are professional musicians who are constantly working elsewhere; indeed, that's why the show at Foo Foo's starts as late as it does; it's because the band have played somewhere else before they get to Dale Street. 'Rockin' Ronnie Ravy, the compère, is in the same boat as the band, inasmuch as he, too, doesn't rely entirely on Foo Foo's for his income. In fact, come to think of it, Michael Ryan, the general manager, is the only one who's employed full-time by the club. Michael, though, has known about the closure for quite a while and consequently (not least because he has a wife and three children to consider) has made contingency plans. His involvement with Monroe's will take up most of his efforts when the club finally closes.

Over the years, I have had many, many memorable nights at Foo Foo's Palace. However, if I was to pick just one as the most memorable, then I'd have to choose Sunday, 24 March 2002. That was the night of my sixty-fifth celebratory gala evening, or, as 'Rockin' Ronnie Ravy put it on the night, 'the landlady's birthday'.

To see some 400 or so special people in the one place – my home – at the one time was a very emotional experience for me. Michael and I chose the guest list personally.

I opened the show as Foo with my theme song, 'I Am What I Am', in a silver gown split to the waist topped off with a huge feather boa. When the Salford Reds rugby league team (dressed in full playing kit) stood behind me on stage and started the first 'Happy Birthday' of the night, then I really did know it was my birthday and thought it was the best present I'd ever had! The rugby players were the beginning of many surprises that night.

After getting changed and coming back on stage as Frank, I was up and down like the proverbial bride's nightie as Ronnie Ravy kept telling me more special guests would like to say a few words and could I leave the stage. It was the first time in 27 years anyone had ever dared say that to me! Among the people who got up and said some very kind words were Susie Mathis, Bryan Robson, Mike Sweeney, Max Beesley, Michael

Le Vell, Vince Miller and Bobby Ball. The very funny Charlie Ale told everyone that I was his father; Maxine Barrie told everyone I was her mother, whilst Joe Longthorne (a man who really does know how to party) treated everyone to a song as only he can. Ryan Giggs then presented me with an enormous card – complete with a marvellous cartoon of me as Foo and Sir Alex Ferguson dressed solely in women's underwear – personally signed by everyone at Old Trafford. Maybe that was the reason Alex was unable to attend! Seriously, though, I did get a note from him apologising for his absence saying he was tied up with business in Coventry.

And then, to cap it all, I got a call from Danny La Rue on my mobile phone. Like everything else on the night, it was a complete surprise and came just as I was going to sing. Danny said some wonderfully kind things to me, things that made me so proud and set the tears off again. It felt so good that the man I'd looked up to and tried to emulate so many years ago could find the time to call me on my special night.

Other guests included all my brothers and nieces and nephews and when I noted the Chief Constable of Manchester, David Wilmott, in the audience, I knew there was no chance of a raid. Phil Neville, Steve Bruce, Garry Pallister and Sam Allardyce also represented the footballing world, along with one full table packed with what looked to me like the whole cast of *Coronation Street*.

It was four of the *Street's* boys who were to provide another surprise. With me once again sitting amongst the audience, the curtain was pulled back to reveal Diana Ross and the Supremes, or, at least, what looked and sounded like them.

Amazingly, it was Simon Gregson (Steve McDonald), Alan Halsall (Tyrone Dobbs) and Sean Wilson (Martin Platt), with Chris Bisson (Vikram Desai) as a fantastic (and very convincing-looking) Diana Ross. I soon shooed him off! On that night of all nights, I wasn't having anyone (especially another man) looking better than me in a frock!

Not surprisingly, we partied until the wee small hours as I tried my utmost to make sure I met everyone who'd kindly turned up. I was quoted in the *Manchester Evening News* the next day as saying, 'It's the best night I've ever had.' Even now, I don't disagree with that comment. It really was a fantastic night and, even if it was a few months early, it was the perfect way to say goodbye to the one and only Foo Foo's Palace.

And so, the story of Frank Pearson and Foo Foo Lammar comes to an end – at least for the time being. It's been a story of contrasts, from handcarts and hand-me-downs to Rolls-Royces and custom-made frocks. It's also been a story of good and bad times, with, fortunately, the good far outweighing the bad. If my next 65 years are as good, I'll have nothing to complain about.